Learn M   e
Step by Step in 7 days for
.NET Developers

By
Saillesh Pawar

FIRST EDITION 2019

Copyright © BPB Publication, INDIA

ISBN: 978-93-88511-38-4

Distributors:

BPB PUBLICATIONS
20, Ansari Road, Darya Ganj
New Delhi-110002
Ph: 23254990/23254991

BPB BOOK CENTRE
376 Old Lajpat Rai Market,
Delhi-110006
Ph: 23861747

MICRO MEDIA
Shop No. 5, Mahendra Chambers,
150 DN Rd. Next to Capital Cinema,
V.T. (C.S.T.) Station, MUMBAI-400 001
Ph: 22078296/22078297

DECCAN AGENCIES
4-3-329, Bank Street,
Hyderabad-500195
Ph: 24756967/24756400

Published by Manish Jain for BPB Publications, 20, Ansari Road, Darya Ganj, New Delhi-110002 and Printed by Repro India Pvt Ltd, Mumbai

Acknowledgments

I would like to express my heartfelt thanks to my Mom and Dad, without their inspiration and support, I might not be the person I am today, and to all those who have been with me in this journey who provided support, read, shared feedback, proofread, and gave their comments.

I am blessed to have my sister Shalini and my brother Rakesh who have always supported me, and my brother-in-law, Dhirender, without their support this journey would have been incomplete.

Special thanks to Mr. Shiv Prasad Koirala who has motivated me since the beginning of my career and pushed me to bring my three months of daily late-night writing to completion. We have finally made it.

Contents

The Era of Data Center

Before the advent of cloud, the business organization would have their business application deployed on the data center.

From Wikipedia:

"A data center (American English or data *center (British English) is a building* or dedicated space within a building used to house *computer systems* and associated components, such as *telecommunications* and *storage systems. It generally includes redundant* or backup components and infrastructure for *power supply, data communications connections, environmental controls (e.g. air conditioning, fire suppression) and various security devices. A large data center is an industrial-scale operation using as much electricity as a small town."*

Image source: https://fortunedotcom.files.wordpress.com/2015/06/ screen-shot-2015-06-24-at-11-54-41-am.png

The approach of data center had many disadvantages for the business organizations. If teams want to increase a ram or storage on the server they have to then go and purchase the computer component. This may take weeks or months.

In .NET technology community, we prefer using Virtual Machine of windows server to host our application on **Internet Information Services (IIS)** web server which runs our web applications. Windows server are more powerful enterprise computer which has powerful computing capabilities i.e. more amount of CPU memory supported, more number of processors, Active Directory, and high availability. So, having a windows server is not only the component required to run a web application, there are also other components required as mentioned as follows:

- IIS installation on server
- Purchasing software licensing (DB license, other third party software license)
- DB server installation (SQL Server, Oracle, etc.)
- **Load Balancer**: Distributes network or application traffic across servers.
- **Cluster Services**: Microsoft Cluster Server allows server computers to work together as cluster to improvise application availability on failover.
- **Procuring Hardware**: Rack mount and Stacking of servers, Operating system installation, Firmware and driver upgradation, RAM to be used by the server and application hosted on server.
- Operating system patch installation
- Antivirus
- **SAN drives**: Storage Area Network provide access to storage devices for server computers.
- **Domain**: Address of your web application through which it will be available on internet.
- **SSL certificate**: Provide secure encrypted communication between a website and browser.
- **SMTP server**: SMTP takes care of email delivery process if used in the web application.
- Network configuration to whitelist IP only for internal access.

All these are tedious and expensive work which may take weeks and sometimes even months. Economically this much time to get the server ready and not utilizing the full resources of server is cost to the company. With the Advent of **Cloud,** the companies pay as per there usage of the server capacity rather than having a full server of their own and not able to use the full resources of a server.

So **Cloud** is basically a third party big vendor which has its own whole lot massive big data center with thousands of servers and the vendor providing the same on rent basis as per our need, so that organization can focus on business rather than computer infrastructure.

Abstract

Cloud Computing has been the hottest discussed topic in the Information Technology world. Each organization wants to leverage the power of the cloud to reduce the maintenance of IT infrastructure cost and increase the ROI on the product and create highly scalable applications like Web application, mobile application, Web APIs, etc. With Cloud computing, there comes various Cloud Service providers which are competing with each other and some new organizations are following the footsteps effectively increasing the competition and providing the alternatives to the customers. E.g.: Azure by Microsoft, Amazon's Web Services, Google, IBM, Oracle, Alibaba etc. In this book, we will be strictly focusing on Microsoft Azure for .NET developers.

Introduction

Azure Cloud is huge and confusing because it has enormous services available to solve your problem in this modern world. Microsoft Azure has Web, Mobile, Big Data, IoT, AI + Machine Learning, Storage, Database etc. We will be going through some of these available services to solve our business problem.

If you are a .NET developer who wants to learn Microsoft Azure and want to have cloud mindset, this book is for you. Cloud application development requires a *Cloud mindset*. Cloud mindset is developed by gradually going through all the available services provided by Microsoft Azure and using the best fit solution for your problem. I have made mistakes while developing Cloud-based solutions and have learned many things from developing the *Cloud Mindset*. We will not be covering the administration part of Azure i.e. how to migrate to cloud, upgrading current azure service virtual machines, Azure active directory, Role Based Access for Azure portal etc.

I hope you have a basic understanding of IIS, C#, Asp.net MVC before going through the next upcoming topics. It's always better to know your weapons before going to a war.

Day 1: Understanding Azure and Services Offered for .NET Developers

Detailing down the number of services offered by Data Center we can conclude them in four different categories which Microsoft Azure provide us.

1. PaaS: Platform as a Service

With PaaS Azure provides us operating system, Web server, DB installed in racks i.e. Azure provides us to build and host our applications without managing the infrastructure, all patch update, antivirus, and other infrastructure related components that are taken care of by Microsoft. E.g.: Cloud Service, Web App and Mobile app as shown in *Figure 1*.

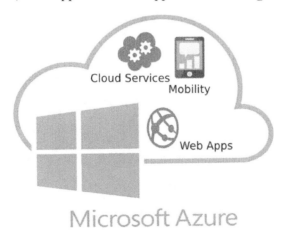

Figure 1 Demonstrating PaaS services provided by Azure

2. IaaS: Infrastructure as a Service

Azure provides storage, networking, servers Virtual Machines on which you have a complete control. With IaaS you are fully responsible for managing everything on your VM from installation of Security patches, Antivirus etc. This Service feels quite similar to our on-premise server where we usually access remote desktop connection and manage our applications. Azure provides VM, Container Instances, Container service in IaaS as shown in Figure 2.

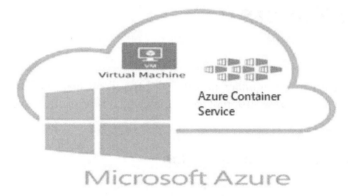

Figure 2 Demonstrating IaaS services provided by Azure

3. SaaS: Software as a Service

SaaS provides users to connect to, and use cloud-based app on the internet like Microsoft office 365 for outlook, Microsoft teams, SharePoint, Calendar, Excel, PowerPoint, Word, Power BI etc. as shown in *Figure 3*.

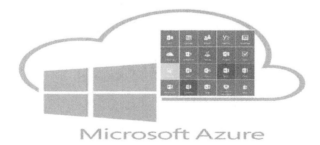

Figure 3 Demonstrating SaaS services provided by Azure

4. LaaS/FaaS: Logic as a Service or Function as a Service

Azure provides us with small fast server-less services to be integrated with various clients. This service can run under pay as you go where you are only charged for the time your function ran. E.g.: Azure Functions and Logic Apps as shown in *Figure 4.*

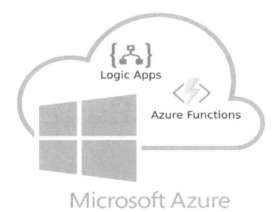

Figure 4 Demonstrating LaaS services provided by Azure

when to use which, among the Services below to solve a problem is a Confusing Task for a developer

As a developer, it's difficult to choose among the above-mentioned services "which to use when" to solve our customer problem. Through various mistakes that I have done while implementing the solution, I have concluded the following description for the above services. There are other services like container services which I will not include in this book. We will be going through each service in detail in the upcoming chapters.

🖳 Azure Virtual Machine

AVM allows us to create a virtual machine which can allow us to run our application on VM. VM can be started and stopped in a couple of minutes. There are various types of images available on Azure Windows, Linux, etc. as shown in Figure 5.

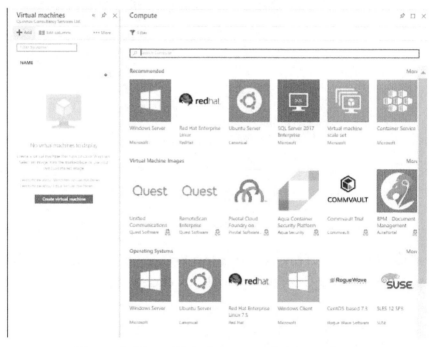

Figure 5 Virtual Machines available on Azure

We can import our own on-premises licenses of SQL server etc. and can be used in VM. We can scale up the VM in case CPU utilization increases. We can choose the VM size as per our configuration which can give full control of everything.

Disadvantage: Slow start and Stop in a couple of minutes.

🏢 Azure Web App for Container

Azure web app for container allow us to use container docker images from docker hub containers and allow your Project code and Docker File to run.

Scale up feature is present. Custom domain and SSL is available.

Azure Service Fabrics

Azure service fabrics allow us to create and deploy micro-services which are easily manageable, updated, and loosely coupled services which are scaled and deployed separately.

Azure Web Apps

Azure web app provides us the capability to create, build and deploy the web, mobile, and API deployment using Microsoft Azure web apps service. In Azure web app we run a web server as a service i.e. we get IIS as a service where we can deploy our APIs, websites.

Web App service Provides:

- Custom Domain
- Deployment Slot to create different slots of the environment which can be swapped in a single click.
- Network and Firewall
- Auto Scale Up feature.
- Deployment of Web, Apis and Web Jobs.
- You just take care of deploying your app and changing your configuration.
- Sandbox security is enabled which take cares of isolating the execution of a web app from other instances. The sandboxing was created to restrict access of shared components i.e. Registry, cryptography, and Graphics.

Note: With my personal experience, if you have a requirement to work with Images, or Pdf creation feature on your app service web application, you need to consider other alternative services.

Web Jobs: To run a background job of type On-Demand, Timer Trigger, Service Bus Trigger Jobs, etc.

Note: We will discuss in depth the Web App and Web Job in upcoming chapters.

Azure Cloud Services

Azure Cloud Services allow us to run and deploy our application on IIS as Web Role and we can run our long-running task scheduler with the help of Worker role as a standalone without any sandbox security. This is similar to our on-premises server where we just let admin team handle OS and framework and patches and we as a developer need to take care of deployment and task schedulers. When the website is facing a huge traffic we can autoscale the website to scale up the instances of web role. Similarly as we can autoscale the worker role instances to process the number messages in the queue if worker role with message queue is implemented. (Note*) – We will talk about this in detail in the upcoming chapters, this is how cloud gives us an edge while developing business solutions.

Allow us to deploy web application via Web Role, API, and Worker Role

Auto Scale feature available.

We have to create a package of web and worker role in order to deploy the app on VM.

We can enable RDP of VM.

Disadvantage: Slow to start and stop, the Deployment process takes a lot of time depending on the size of package created of the application solution.

Azure Function

The azure function is fast light-weighted server less logic which executes a small piece code and fits in following scenarios i.e. Processing on event streams (IOT, event hub), Web API (Http Trigger Azure function), Publisher and Subscriber jobs e.g.: sending a message to the queue, generating event base on storage event, running a job on-demand, creating small logic APIs.

The azure function can be a trigger on the timer trigger basis. For long running stateful task we can use durable functions.

Azure Logic Apps

Azure Logic App is a kind of workflow logic where we drag and drop the workflow for our business requirement. The azure logic app doesn't require the knowledge of coding, hence saves a lot of development time.

The app can be quickly published and easy to maintain.

Allows Timer Schedule Trigger, HTTP & API Trigger

Polling Trigger Service Bus queue, Azure Queue, and so on.

Azure Logic App is based on the event and will execute an action based on the workflow designer.

So now you would be able to differentiate between above services provided by Azure and when to use which for deploying and building your web app, mobile, and APIs on Azure.

In our next chapter, we will look at how we can register for free Azure account and start our journey as .NET cloud developer.

Day 2: Creating Your Free Microsoft Azure Account and Create your First Web App Service on Microsoft Azure

Before diving in: In order to leverage the Azure power, we need to have an account on Azure Portal. In this chapter, we will create our free Azure subscription step by step and then, walk through the web app service and Apis overview on the web portal.

Create Your Free Azure Trial Account

Step1: Go to https://azure.microsoft.com/en-in/free/

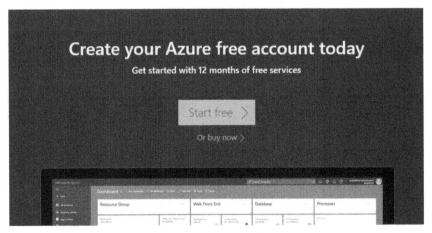

Figure 6 Azure free account homepage

Step2: Click on **Start free** button.

Step3: You will need to have Microsoft account in order to register. This will take a couple of minutes if you don't have one. If you already have the account, you can just login into your account.

Step4: Enter your new email.

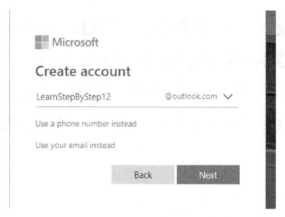

Figure 7 Creating your free Azure Account

Step5: Enter your password.

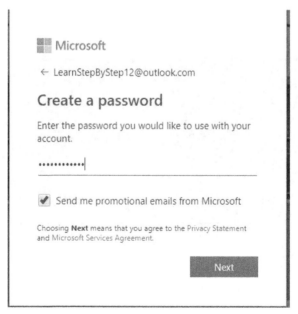

Figure 8 User Enters the Password for Azure

Step 6: Click on **Next**.

Step 7: Enter Captcha value:

Figure 9 User Enters the Captcha

Step 8: Now start the free Azure registration as shown in the following screenshot:

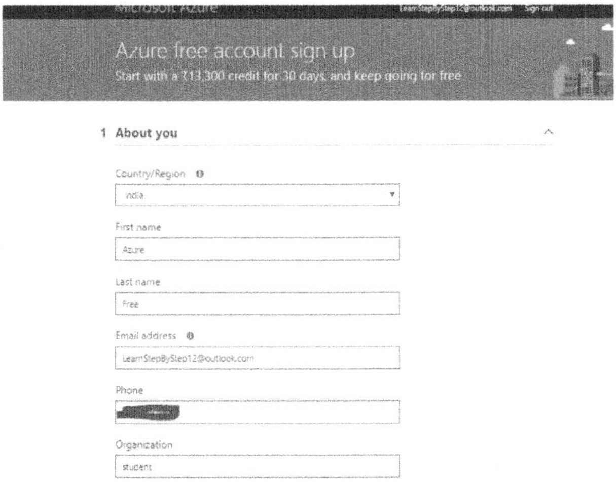

Figure 10 User filling the Registration form

If you are trying to register on Azure from India you need to enter your PAN details then click next.

Step 9: Enter your phone number to validate and then enter your credit card details. Once your 30 days are over this account will automatically get deactivated so no need to worry about.

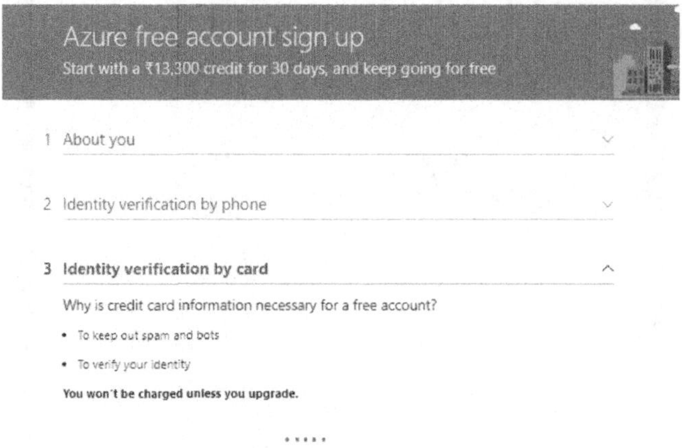

Figure 11 Validating User verification

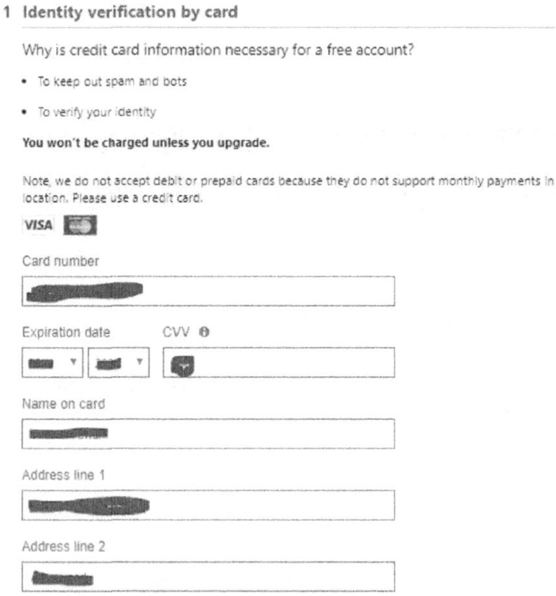

Figure 12 User inputting credit card information

Step 10: Click **Next**.

Step 11: Agree to the Agreement clause as shown below and you are good to go:

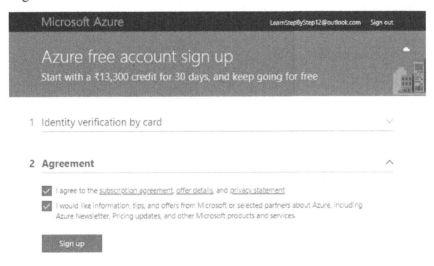

Figure 13 User accepts the Agreement

Once you are done below popup will show. Pop Up shows you about your free services and how you can manage your free account in a better way.

Figure 14 Recommendations for users

You can skip this part if this is getting more overwhelming to follow all the steps. If you want to check your credit limit, you can see the below notification which triggers once you create your free account.

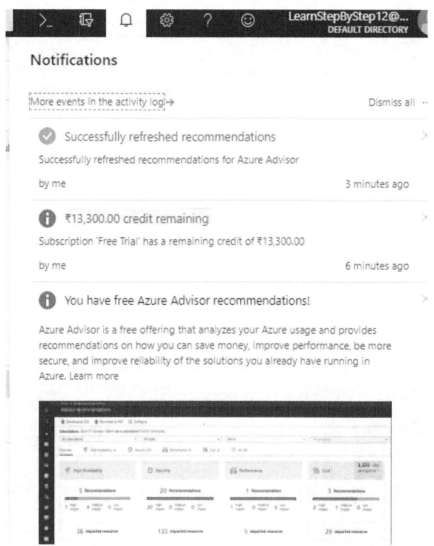

Figure 15 Successfully account creation

Create your First Web App Service on Azure

Resource Group

Before directly jumping in and creating web app resource, let's first discuss how we do software development in real life. We all have a certain working environment for deploying our web application like Dev, QA, UAT, Pre-Production, and Prod. These environments have their own separate sets of software installed, which are independent of each environments i.e. SQL Server, IIS, Storage, load balancer, cluster services, Redis cache server, etc. So, before we go and start deploying our application on Microsoft Azure, We need a resource group which we need to configure before deploying any application that will either be used by us or by the customers. In Azure, we have a concept of Resource Groups which are environments where we actually have a set of resources particularly assigned to an Environment like Dev, QA, UAT, and Production. It helps us with all our respective environment resources being grouped to the particular resource group and you can manage your groups by adding any resource to the group you want.

We can add a Resource Group while adding different service type to

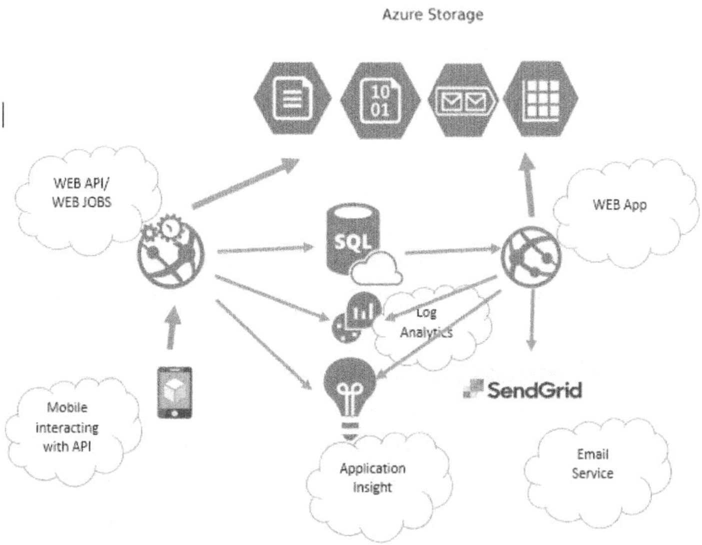

Figure 16 Resource Group container

our subscription. We will see once we will work with web app service on Azure. Below is the small resource group container explaining an application where mobile is communicating with Web API app service and storing the data in SQL server. We also have another Web APP which is reading from this DB and showing to the user and there are other resources consumed by the application.

Adding a Resource Group

For enterprise application and automation normally we create resources via ARM template i.e. Azure Resource Manager template via Azure CLI, Visual Studio, and PowerShell or bash for windows (Automation). In this book we will be creating resource group from Azure Portal which is actually manual way of creating Azure resources.

1. Go to your Azure portal and Login into your account.
2. Click on Resource Groups Icon.

Figure 17 Creating Azure Resource Group

3. It will ask for our Resource Name. We can give it a name as per our environment-product name. So I will be naming it **dev-LearnAzureStepByStep**.

4. **Subscription**: A user can have more than one subscription. Projects that you're developing, one for each Subscription (per customer/client). A company can divide their subscription by department name as well. We will be using the free trial subscription that we just subscribed.

5. **Resource Group Location**: Resource group location specifies that in which location you want to create these resources? We can choose the

region as per client requirement whichever is near to client/customer location. I will choose Central India as of now and click on **Create**.

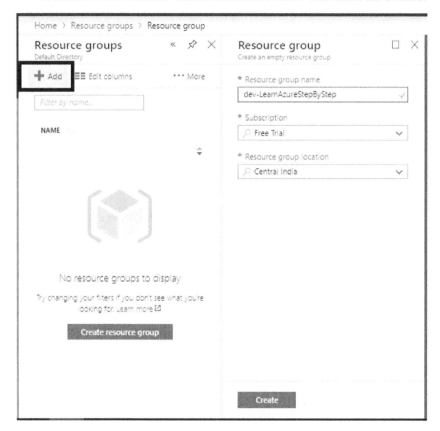

Figure 18 Configuring Azure Resource Group

Once we are done with creating our resource group. On any action taken on Azure Portal we get a notified toaster popup showing that your action has been completed, this basically informs each and every activity that is being performed on Azure portal.

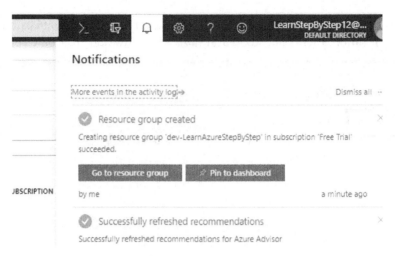

Figure 19 Successfully created Azure Resource Group

We can pin the resource to the dashboard so that we can create a shortcut of that resource on our dashboard and visit our resource group as shown in the following screenshot:

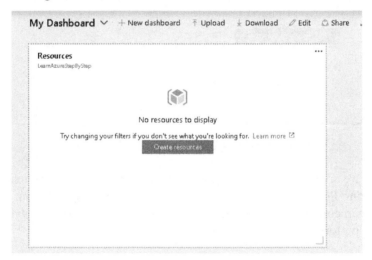

Figure 20 Pinning Resource Group in dashboard

Now we are done with resource group let's get started and add a Web App service on our resource group.

Creating a Web App Service Resource on your Subscription

1. Click on **Create resources**.

Figure 21 Create Web App on Azure

We can also create a resource from our resource group as well as shown below, in case you skipped to add resource group shortcut on the dashboard.

Figure 22 Create Web App on Azure from Resource Group

2. Search for Web App.

So now my business requirement says that they don't want to take care about underlining infrastructure related stuff, they just want web application running. Keeping this in mind, we can go for Web App as a Service where we just have to care about the deployment and Microsoft will take care of the entire infrastructure.

Figure 23 Selecting Web App Service

Figure 24 Creating Web App Service

As you can see in the above figure we get many options available as a .NET developer. In this chapter, we will only focus on deploying Web app Service plan without any backend DB to Azure. As we can see there is an option as Web App + SQL which we will look into in our upcoming chapters.

Select Web App and click on **Create**:

Once you are done, it will ask for the below details:

Attribute Name:

1. **App Name**: App Name textbox specifies the name of your application.
2. **Subscription**: Type of subscription plan that you want to billed
3. **Resource Group**: In which resource group this resource should be added. I have added the resource to our Dev resource group.

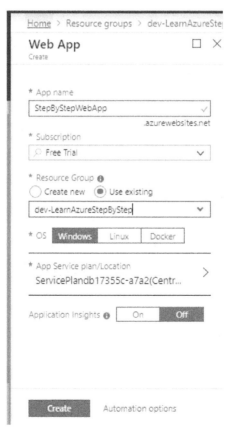

Figure 25 Creating Web App Service

4. **Operating System**: Windows, we can also use Docker and Linux to run our ASP.NET Core app.

5. **App Service Plan**: Plan for your web app which is actually the hardware capacity of the App Service. This may vary as per your usage.

6. **Application Insight**: Used to trace in-depth analysis of your website performance, issues etc.

Click on **Create** button. It will take a few seconds to create your web app resource and then you are ready to go. Now, once our resource gets created we will go to the resource group and we can see our Web App is successfully created as shown in the following figure:

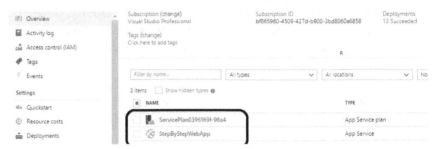

Figure 26 Successfully created Azure App Service

Click on your resource, and let's investigate what other features it provides.

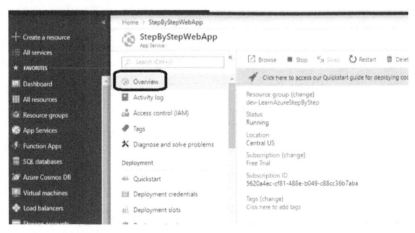

Figure 27 Overview of Azure App Service

We can see in the border region their various APIs given by azure to control your Web App, we will discuss some of the important APIs over here.

1. **Overview Dashboard**: Provides us with all our Web app details and various APIs to configure our Web App as mentioned below:
   (a) **Browse**: Open your website on the browser
   (b) **Stop**: Stop your web app
   (c) **Restart**: Restart your web app
   (d) **Delete**: Delete the resource
   (e) **Get Publish profile**: Profile to deploy your website on Azure
   (f) Reset the publish profile
   (g) Our Resource Group name where web app belongs to
   (h) **Status**: Stopped or Running
   (i) **URL**: Our application URL you can click and check your application.
   (j) **Location**: Region location
   (k) **Ftp Deployment**: Enabled or not?
   (l) **Ftp Details**: Hostname
   (m) Subscription ID

Figure 28 Navigation to App Service Url

Other API Details:

- **Activity Log:** Gives the details of your activities on your subscription for the particular resource.
- **Access Control**: You can grant and block access to this resource for other users if you want, so that other Azure user would not be able to access this resource.
- **Deployment Credentials:** If you want to deploy your website via FTP you need to configure the username and password for the same.
- **Deployment slots:** The Deployment slots are used to create different slots of a website with zero downtime deployment, so you can create

your website and test the same on slot 2. Once you are done testing your application you can change the slot. Your Slot 2 web app will be swapped to slot1 which will be public facing URL. You can achieve zero downtime deployment with this.

- **Deployment option:** If you want to deploy your web app from source control you can configure the same on this landing page.

- **Application Setting:** Application setting just like **AppSettings** in **web.config** that you want your application to use.

- **Scale up:** Scale up means when you need to upgrade your hardware capacity you want to give more resources to your server (Allocating more CPU, more memory). When you are hitting your selected quota, you can choose as per your environment.

- **Scale Out:** Scale out means more servers, basically deploying your website on multiple servers and creating a load balancer to distribute the traffic between them. Load balance is already provided by the platform.

- **Web Jobs:** Web Jobs are used for long background task which we will discuss in our next chapter.

- **Advance Tool:** This navigates us to KUDU that has a lot of hidden feature which will help us to see all the directories structure and where our application is deployed. We will dig into kudu in the upcoming chapters.

- **App Service Editor**: It is quite helpful when you deploy your app and want to edit your **web.config** on your respective environment.

In the next chapter, we will learn how to create a simple Web App and deploy our Web App on Azure using Visual Studio.

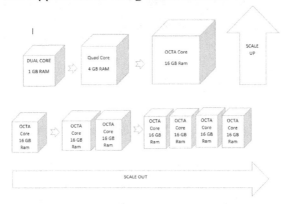

Figure 29 Scale Up and Scale Out

Day 3: Creating and Deploying a Sample ASP.NET Core App with SQL Server to Azure

Before diving in: In this chapter, we will create and deploy a sample ASP. NET core app on Azure. We will then deploy our already working web application on Azure with SQL Azure DB.

Creating a Sample ASP.NET Core App Step by Step

In the previous chapter, we successfully created our Web App service on Azure. Let's start creating our app and deploy it on Web App service.

Create a sample ASP.NET Core application step by step. I will be using Visual Studio 2017 for developing and writing a demo. VS2017 has all the SDK for Azure, I will suggest you download the community edition from the following link.

https://visualstudio.microsoft.com/vs/community/

So let's get started.

Creating your Sample ASP.NET Core application:

1. Open Visual Studio
2. Create New Project

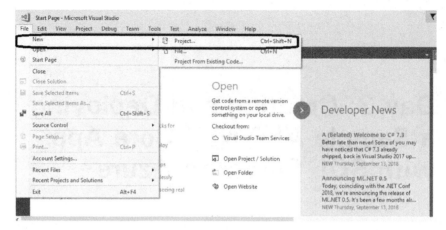

Figure 30 Creating a new project in Visual Studio

3. Name your Project as AzureStepbyStep

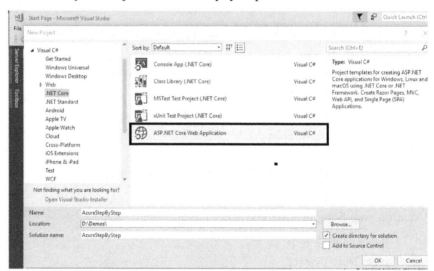

Figure 31 Select ASP.NET Core Project

4. Click on **OK** and select Web Application ASP.NET MVC.

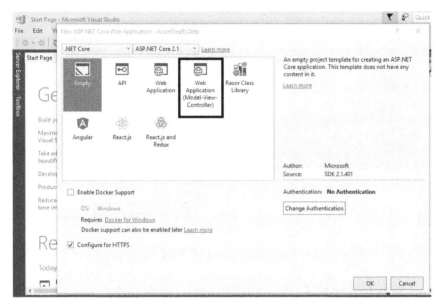

Figure 32 Select MVC template

5. Once your project is created, build and run it on your local environment first to test whether everything is working fine or not?

Figure 33 Successfully created our first ASP.NET Core project

6. Press **F5** and check the Homepage of your sample website.

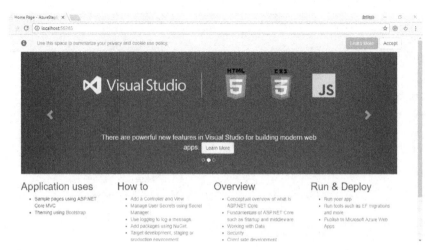

Figure 34 Running our ASP.NET Core project

Our Sample ASP.NET Core is up and running. Now let's not waste our time and deploy the same on Azure.

In order to deploy the same on our Development environment, I will go to my Azure portal and download the publish profile from my web app resource as shown in the following screenshot:.

Figure 35 Downloading Web app publish profile

Usually real life Deployment these days are done via continuous integration and continuous deployment tools like Team City, VSTS etc., but in this journey we will be deploying everything from Visual Studio. Once you have downloaded the development published profile we will go and publish our website from the Visual studio via import publish profile feature in Visual Studio. You can follow the below mentioned steps.

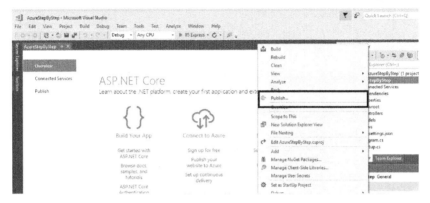

Figure 36 Publishing Web app from Visual Studio

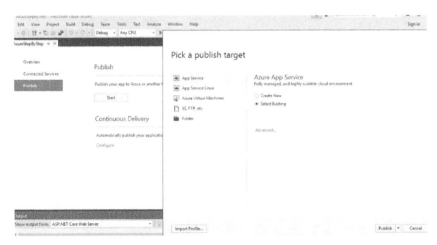

Figure 37 Selecting the Existing App Service

Click on **Import Profile**.

Once you select the publish profile, your first deployment on Azure will start. Visual Studio will connect to FTP details present in publishing profile file which is basically an XML file with all the details about where to deploy our web app.

Deployment process may vary according to the size of the application. Once the deployment process is completed, visual studio will automatically

navigate you to your website URL e.g. http://stepbystepwebapp.
azurewebsites.net/

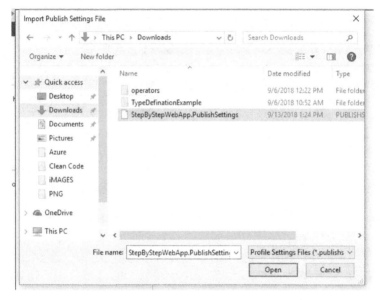

Figure 38 Importing the downloaded publish profile of web app

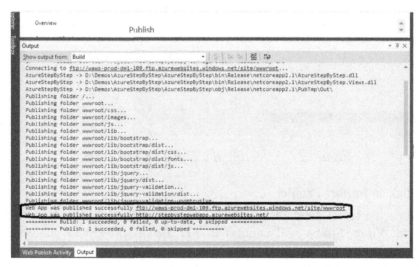

Figure 39 Publish status in Visual studio

You can see our sample ASP.NET core app running on Azure.

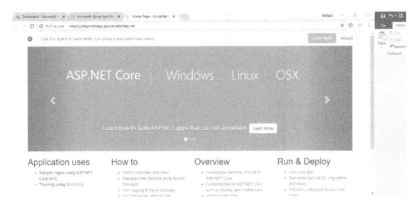

Figure 40 Successfully published our ASP.NET Core web app

You can see how easy it is to create our Resource Group by simply following the steps one by one and then as per our sample web application requirement we choose web app service and deployed our web application successfully.

So now let's add a backend database to our current project. For demonstrating the DB part I will create a Customer registration page in our application and save the details on SQL server on Azure. In order to save the details we need to have SQL Server on Azure, let's first create SQL Server on Azure.

Everything

Filter

sql server

NAME	PUBLISHER	CATEGORY
SQL Server 2016 SP1 Enterprise on Windows Server 2016	Microsoft	Compute
SQL server (logical server)	Microsoft	Databases
SQL Server Module	Microsoft	Databases
DgSecure for SQL Server	Dataguise	Compute
ScaleArc for SQL Server	ScaleArc	Compute
SQL Server AlwaysOn Cluster	Microsoft	Compute
ScaleArc for SQL Server (pay-go)	ScaleArc	Compute

Figure 41 Searching a SQL Server resource on Azure

Creating a SQL Server Resource on Azure Step by Step

1. Login to your Azure free account.
2. Go to our resource group which we created in Chapter 2. i.e. **dev-LearnAzureStepByStep**
3. Add a new resource as SQL Server.
4. Click on **Create**.

Figure 42 Creating a SQL Server resource on Azure

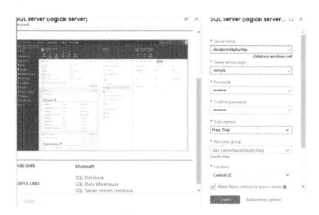

Figure 43 Configuring SQL Server resource on Azure

5. Add SQL server details like username, a credential which we will use to login to our SQL Server. This will create our SQL Server resource which we will be using in our application.

Figure 44 Selecting SQL server for configuration

Click on SQL Server resource, and let's create a new Database for our application.

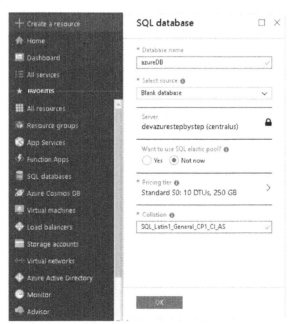

Figure 45 Configuring SQL Server datebase on Azure

Attribute for Database creation:

1) Name your database name.

2) Select source i.e. sample adventure work DB or backup DB.

3) **SQL elastic pool**: Select not now this used for dynamic resource allocation i.e. if your DB is consuming peak usage DB gets the performance resource they need.

4) Select Pricing tier as **Basic**.

5) Click on **OK**.

You will get the toaster notification:

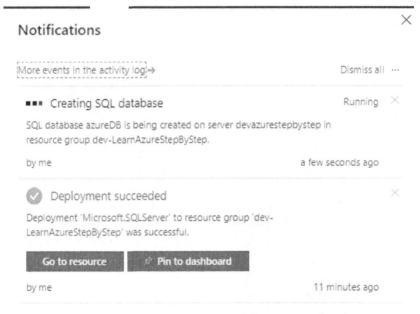

Figure 46   Azure creating our SQL Server database

Once you get Notification as successfully created SQL Server. Go to resource group again or you can directly go to SQL Databases menu for a shortcut.

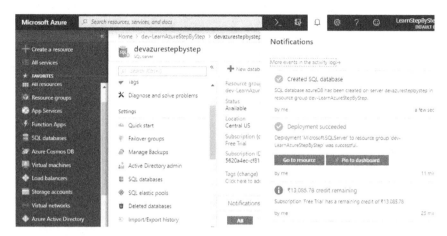

Figure 47 Successfully created Azure database

Click on SQL databases link, then you will see newly created Dev DB by us as shown in the following screenshot:

Figure 48 Our new created SQL server database

Click on **AzureDB**.

Connect to Azure SQL Database from SSMS

1. Open SQL Server Management Studio.
2. Copy Server Name from Azure Db overview page in SSMS as shown in the following screenshot:

Figure 49 Server Name of our database

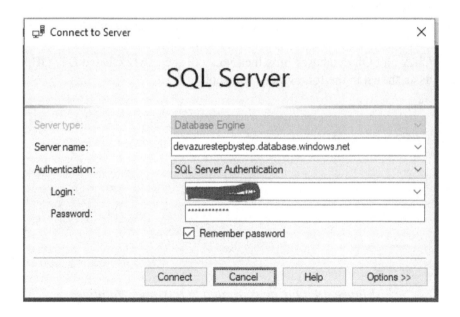

Figure 50 Connecting Azure database using SSMS

3. You will be prompted with the following popup.

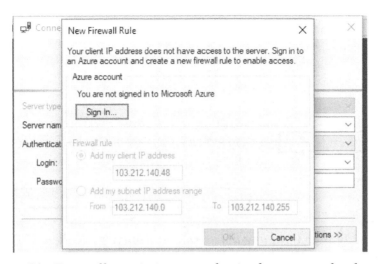

Figure 51 Firewall restricting unauthorized access to database

4. This message tells us that our IP has not been whitelisted to access the Azure DB.

5. Go to SQL Server resource we created and click on **Firewalls and Virtual Network**.

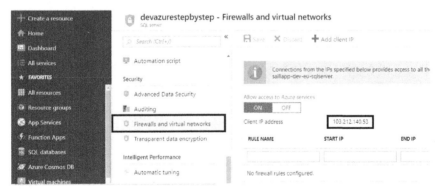

Figure 52 Whitelisting User IP address

6. I will add my name as Rule and my IP address as mentioned in the popup.

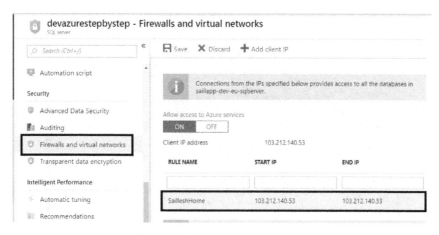

Figure 53 Adding a new rule to whitelist the client IP

Save the changes. Toaster message will come that your changes have been saved successfully. Now let's connect to the SQL server again.

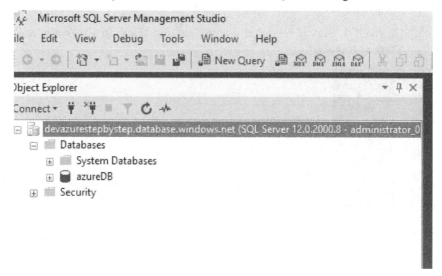

Figure 54 Successfully connected to AzureDb

Now you can see that we are now able to connect to our SQL server and we can see our azureDB created on SQL server.

I will use Entity Framework Core to connect to my SQL server database. You can see the migrations and code changes in the project in the bitbucket/ Github repository which I will share in later references. For now, I will share the snapshot of my sample migration. In our application I have added a Customer form which I am going to save in DB.

```
PM> Add-Migration InitialCreate
The EF Core tools version '2.1.1-rtm-30846' is older than that of the runtime '2.1.3-rtm-32065'. Update the
tools for the latest features and bug fixes.
To undo this action, use Remove-Migration.
PM> Update-Database
The EF Core tools version '2.1.1-rtm-30846' is older than that of the runtime '2.1.3-rtm-32065'. Update the
tools for the latest features and bug fixes.
```

Figure 55 Adding migration for the database

```
PM> Update-Database
The EF Core tools version '2.1.1-rtm-30846' is older than that of the runtime '2.1.3-rtm-32065'. Update the
tools for the latest features and bug fixes.
Applying migration '20180915123551_InitialCreate'.
Done.
PM> |
```

Figure 56 Applying migration on database

Now we will check whether our migration was successfully created on our Azure DB or not as shown in the following screenshot:

Figure 57 Showing the migration successfully executed on SQL Server

We can see the Entity framework migration table has been created along with our Customers table. Now we are ready to run our web app on the local environment and check whether the details are getting saved or not. Run the application on localhost.

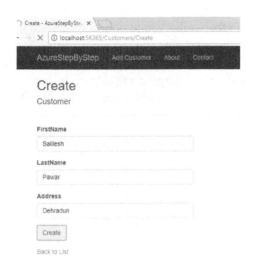

Figure 58 UI showing Create Customer Form

Enter your details on the Customer form and click on **Create** button.

Figure 59 UI showing Customer Lists Form

Bingo: You can see our application is successfully interacting with our Azure DB. Let us now deploy our App on Azure and see whether our application is able to access our DB on Azure and access our website on the Internet. We will follow the same steps that we followed in starting of our chapter i.e. publishing via publishing profile that we have already downloaded.

Let's start with publishing our website and then access it.

Note: If you are using any logging framework or other types which keeps locking any IO device it's recommended to stop your web app first and then start deploying.

Once the deployment is completed visual studio navigates to the website URL as shown in the following screenshot:

Figure 60 Successfully deployed the changes to our Application

We can see that our changes have been successfully deployed on Azure and now we can access our customer form page.

Let's go and test our application and check whether everything is working fine or not. In order to test the same I will create one more customer as shown in the following screenshot:

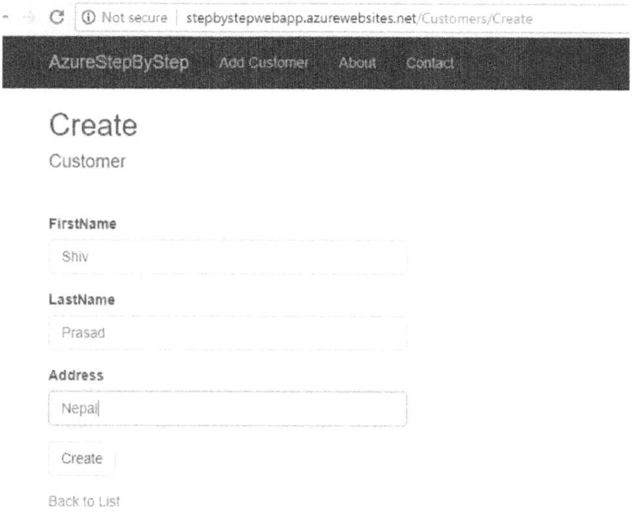

Figure 61 Creating Customer from live Azure website

Save the new Customer and our application will show two customers now as shown in the following screenshot:

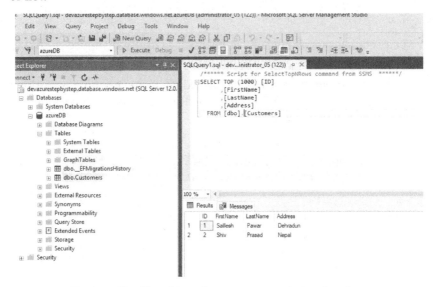

Figure 62 UI showing Customer List from database

Let's go and check our DB whether these records are present over there or not.

Figure 63 Checking the new records in database

From the above records we can see how easily we created Web App on Azure then we created our sample web application in Visual Studio 2017 to be deployed on Azure. Once we successfully deployed the Web App we then created our SQL Server on Azure along with DB and finally we deployed a full working customer facing User Interface and DB integrated Web Application on Azure.

Day 4: Creating and Running a Background Job with Help of Web Jobs on Azure

Before diving in: As I mentioned earlier in our first chapter it is important to have a cloud mindset while developing Cloud based applications. Today we will go through Web Jobs and how you can create a background job or Task Scheduler Job which we deployed on our on premise server with the help of Web Jobs on Azure and see what scaling up instances mean on Web Job and how to create high-performance web jobs.

Web Jobs

Normally in order to solve business problems, we tend to create a lot of small Task Schedulers which basically have some business logic to be run for e.g.:

- Updating DB Records based on some logic
- Moving processed files to success folder
- Sending mail to users

I believe we all have been doing this and this has been close to our heart. Anytime the requirement comes where we have to do a task on daily basis at a particular time we just create an EXE and schedule via Task Schedulers. But now we are using Azure Web Apps and we don't have a dedicated server to run our Task Scheduler to run our jobs. So in order to run a Task on Web Apps, we have **Web Jobs**.

Web Jobs are of two types:

Timer Triggered

- Triggered at a particular time

- Can be trigger by the user manually

Continuous Running

- Continuous Running Jobs are those Web Jobs which are continuously listening to events like message on the queue, file uploaded on blob storage, and any record added on cosmos.
1. Service Bus triggered Note: We will talk about this in details when we create a Service Bus triggered web job.
2. Blob upload Event trigger: Whenever a file is uploaded on blob storage.
3. This is feature of Cloud where you can run multiple instance of your logic parallel for processing faster and quickly. Singleton instance can be configured from the configuration.
4. Background Services run and invoke the job when needed.

Note: Web jobs run on the same stack of your web app i.e. it takes the resources of your web app.

Advantages:

1. Lightly weighted framework, fast to deploy and restart the job as compared to Worker Role (we will be covering worker role in the upcoming chapter).
2. Can run multiple instances of web jobs parallel in order to fasten the process.
3. Good for running the long running tasks.

Case Study: Reading File from FTP server for different clients using Web Job

So as per Case Study, there are various different clients admin who will first configure/Save the FTP details via a web application and save FTP configuration in the DB.

All Clients have automated CSV file upload to their FTP server, you have to create a web job to read the file and process it in DB.

Timer Trigger Job will read all clients FTP details from DB and send these detail one by one in a message queue with the client identifier.

Service Bus Trigger Job will automatically trigger with the message send by Timmer Trigger job and you can then read the file from Client FTP server and process it in DB. Web job will process the messages parallel.

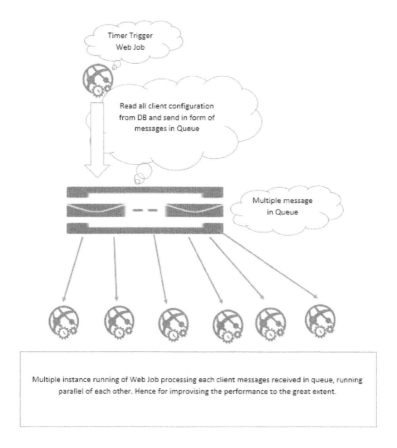

Figure 64 Case Study

Creating Your First Timer Trigger Web Job Using VS 2017

So now we will be creating a timer triggered web job, which executes after every one hour and counts the number of the user registered on our website in Console window. We will add a web job project (web job SDK) to our existing web app project and deploy them at the same time on Azure. As we have mentioned above, web job uses the resources of the web app, so they can be deployed along with the web app.

1. Open Project solution of Azure Step by Step.

2. Click on **Solution** and add a new project.

3. Select Azure Web Job.

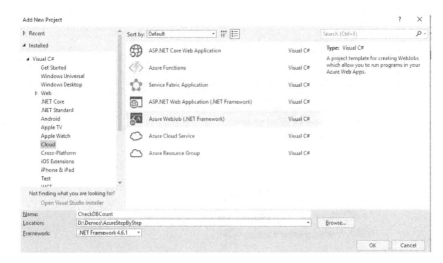

Figure 65 Selecting Azure WebJob Project template

4. Click **OK**.

Understanding the Web Job solution structure

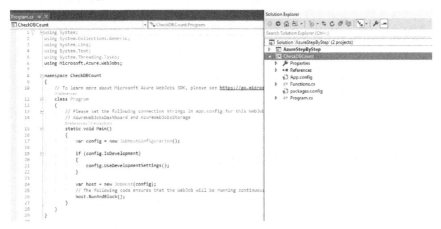

Figure 66 Web Job Project structure

5. Web Job is a kind of a console application only that we used to create for our task scheduler.

   1. **Program.cs** is the entry point of the application, let's go with the code, what does what?

1) **JobHostConfiguration** is used to configure our web job i.e. what kind of job is it? Is it a Timer Triggered, Service Triggered Job etc.

2) **JobHost** is a kind of while (true) loop which keeps the job running and didn't stop the job until we stop it. So that it can be invoked by background services to run at a certain time interval.

3) **Functions** is the Actual code which will get executed each time the Web Job gets triggered.

4) **App.Config** to store configuration details used in the application.

5) **Pacakges.config** Nuget packages installed in our current nugget project.

```
Functions.cs + X  Program.cs
CheckDBCount                              CheckDBCount.Functions          ProcessQueueMe
     1     using System;
     2     using System.Collections.Generic;
     3     using System.IO;
     4     using System.Linq;
     5     using System.Text;
     6     using System.Threading.Tasks;
     7     using Microsoft.Azure.WebJobs;
     8
     9     namespace CheckDBCount
    10     {
                 0 references
    11         public class Functions
    12         {
    13             // This function will get triggered/executed when a new message is written
    14             // on an Azure Queue called queue.
                     0 references | 0 exceptions
    15             public static void ProcessQueueMessage([QueueTrigger("queue")] string message, TextWriter log)
    16             {
    17                 log.WriteLine(message);
    18             }
    19         }
    20     }
    21
```

Figure 67 Demonstrating Function which will get a trigger when there is any message in a queue called Queue

The function is basically a code block which gets executed each time when the job is run so your main logic remains inside the function. For now, let's remove this code and add our Timer trigger code because we are creating a Timer Trigger job.

In order to get dependency related to Timer Trigger jobs, install below NuGet package on your web job project else Timer Trigger dependency won't come.

Microsoft.Azure.WebJobs 3.0.2

Once done, set your code on **Program.cs** as shown in the following screenshot:

```
class Program
    {// Please set the following connection strings in app.config for this WebJob
to run:
        // AzureWebJobsDashboard and AzureWebJobsStorage
        static void Main()
        {var config = new JobHostConfiguration();
            config.UseTimers();
            var host = new JobHost(config);
// The following code ensures that the WebJob will be running continuously
            host.RunAndBlock();
        }
    }
```

In Function class add the following code:

```
public static void Process([TimerTrigger("*/5 * * * * *",RunOnStartup =true)]
TimerInfo timer, TextWriter log)
    {

    }
```

Here Timer Trigger attribute contains a CRON Expression of Time. The above-mentioned CRON expression is for Every five seconds. You can learn about CRON Expression and describing the CRON expression from the following URL:

- https://cronexpressiondescriptor.azurewebsites.net
- https://crontab.guru/
- https://codehollow.com/2017/02/azure-functions-time-trigger-cron-cheat-sheet/

So now in order to implement the logic to show registered users, we need to communicate with DB. In order to do so I will use Entity Framework Core to interact with DB to fasten the process of getting customer details from the database.

Set **CheckDBCount** project as startup project to test your first web job on the local environment.

Before running application, I want you to focus on **app.config** connection string attribute mentioned as follows:

```
<add name="AzureWebJobsDashboard" connectionString="" />
  <add name="AzureWebJobsStorage" connectionString="" />
```

- **AzureWebJobsDashboard** is the storage account used by web job to store logs.

- **AzureWebJobsStorage** is the storage account used to store application-related data e.g. tables, file storage, blog storage (we will look into this in upcoming topics).

Let's create Azure Storage on our resource group so that we can use that configuration in our project as shown in the following screenshot figure:

6. Go to the resource group and add storage account or you can directly go to the storage account and click on add.

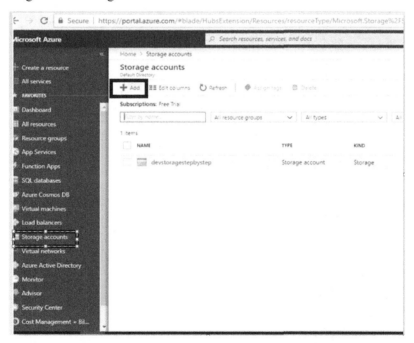

Figure 68 Adding a Storage Account on Azure

Azure Storage is itself a very vast topic which we will not cover in this book. In an abstract way we need storage to store our Non-Relational or Relational data that may be files, images etc. Azure provides us Azure Storage to deal with Storage as we don't have our normal Hard Drives on Web app.

Various Storage Types:

- **File Storage** used to store files like text, etc.
- **Blob Storage** used store complex, unstrcutured files like Json, images, audio etc.
- **Table Storage:** used to data in a tabular format Non-relational.
- **SQL Datbases:** SQL Server relational DB.
- **Cosmos DB:** Un-Structured Document based DB.
- **Queue Storage:** used to store small messages to communicate between publisher and subscriber model.

Figure 69 Configuring Storage Account on Azure

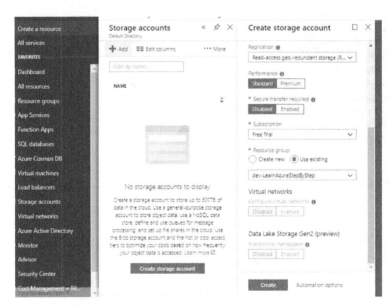

Figure 70 Creating Storage Account on Azure

Configure your Azure storage as shown in the above figures.

Click on **Create**. Once done, go to the resource group than go to your created storage.

Figure 71 Successfully created storage account on Azure

7. Usually, in windows server, we have dedicated storage drives like D, H etc. But on Azure web App we don't have any concept of storage drive. We have to use Azure Storage and need to have Azure Storage account. So in case you want to store any files in any folder you need to save them in Azure file storage. We will discuss Storage in details in our upcoming topics.

8. Get the configuration details of storage account from access key option on overview window of storage account.

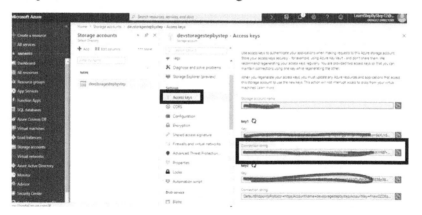

Figure 72 Extracting the storage account details from Azure

Copy connection string and paste inside the connection string of **AzureWebJobsStorage** and **AzureWebJobsDashboard** save it in **app. config** of our Web job.

Figure 73 Using extracted account configuration details in App.config

So now we are ready and all is set up to run our first Web Job on our local machine. Press *F5* button and run.

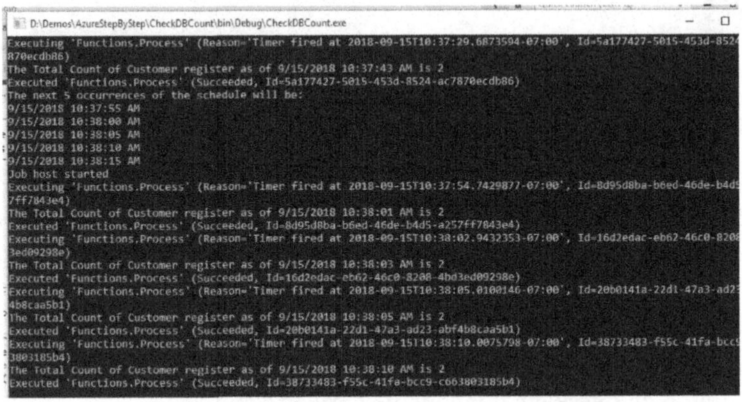

Figure 74 Running your first Web Job

Figure 75 Illustrating configuring the time in App.config

We can clearly see in the above Figure in the five occurrences of the schedule where it's mentioned job will get triggered after every five seconds and display the number of registered user in our DB. You can download the source code from references containing each project.

Tip: We can set the Timer Cron expression on **app.config** so that it's configurable, as shown in the following screenshot:

Deploying Web job on Azure

1. Right click on **CheckDBCount** project and click on **Publish as Azure Website**.

Figure 76 Publish our first Web job on Azure

2. We will be running this Web Job on demand so set run mode as **Run on Demand**.

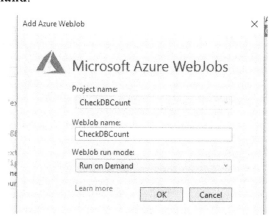

Figure 77 Selecting Web job run mode as Run on Demand

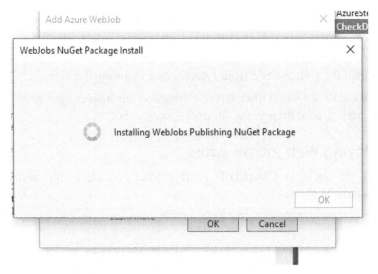

Figure 78 Publish process initiates

Import same publish Profile used by your web app. As we have already
discussed Web Job uses the same resources used by our web app so we
need to deploy with the same profile, until you want to use the separate
web app for web jobs only.

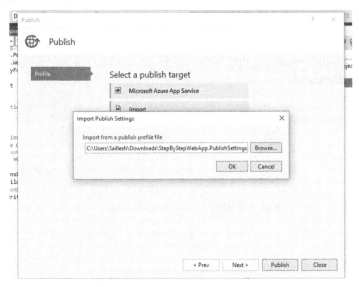

Figure 79 Importing publish profile to publish web job on Azure

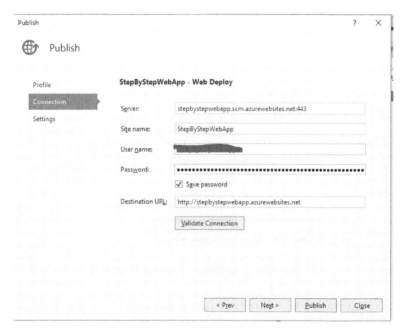

Figure 80 Successfully imported publish profile

Click on **Publish**. Visual Studio will now publish our web job on Azure. Once Visual studio prompts publish successfully. Open Azure portal and get to the web app and click on Web Jobs option in feature section as shown below:

Figure 81 Successfully published Web job on Azure

We can see that our web job has been deployed successfully. As we have set **RunOnStartup** as true, the job would have triggered once, but still we would run it again manually.

Checking Console Log of Web Job:

- Select the job for which you want to check logs as shown in the following screenshot:

Figure 82 Checking logs of Web Job

Click on the prompt Logs option. It will navigate us to logs Page where we can see our console log written as shown in the following screenshot:

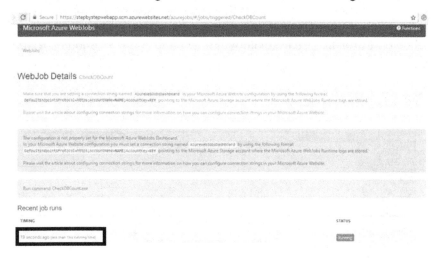

Figure 83 All Web jobs will be listed here

Click on Timing 19 Seconds link and a Toggle Output window will appear as shown in the following screenshot:

Figure 84 Click on Toggle Output to see the console logs

Click on **Toggle Output**:

Figure 85 Downloading the console logs

Here we can see our console log and we can confirm that our job is running fine as per our expectation. If we want to download the whole console logs we can click on download option as shown in the above figure.

Figure 86 Demonstrating Downloaded console output file

Stopping Timer Triggered Jobs

As of now, there are no options to stop a timer trigger job. You can do this by adding the following configuration on azure app settings options to stop timer trigger jobs.

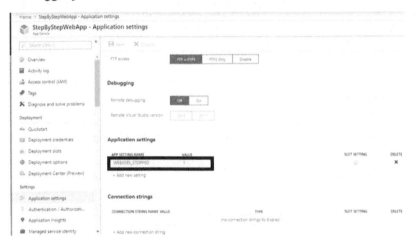

Figure 87 Stopping Web job on Azure

As this chapter is getting longer, we have separated the Service Bus Trigger Web Job in Chapter *Day5*. As of now try practicing the Timer Trigger Web Job and not worry about Service Bus trigger Web Jobs.

Day 5: Creating and Running a Service Bus Triggered Web Jobs on Azure to Send Mail to the Customer using Send Grid

Before diving in this chapter, we will continue with our Web Job topic and extend our web job with Event based trigger i.e. Publisher and Subscriber model. In the chapter, we will be creating a job with real-life practical scenario where we have to send mail to users based on business requirement. We will be using Send Grid service to send mail to the registered customers.

Service Bus Trigger Jobs

Usually, I create Service Bus Trigger job because these jobs are easy to execute. Service Bus trigger jobs work on Publisher and Subscriber model where Client publishes some messages on to the Queue and we have a job which acts as a Subscriber (listening) to that queue. So, if any message comes into the queue the job automatically get triggered as demonstrated in figure:

With the above-shown figure, you should be able to understand how Publisher and Subscriber model works. I have been using these models intensively in our Project. Our Publisher was sometimes Web application when I wanted to run a long-running task. The web application will send a message to a specific queue and our web job will get triggered as soon as it gets invoked. Apart from this we have been using an Azure function to send a message to the queue to invoke our web job on an On-Demand perspective. Whenever we want to run any job, we would run Azure function manually, this would trigger the message to the queue and our web job will get invoked.

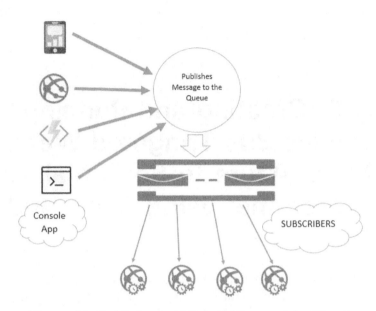

Figure 88 Publisher and Subscriber model of Service Bus Trigger Jobs

In order to implement the same, I would suggest some tools which I highly recommend and use while creating a service bus trigger web jobs. Basically, I heavily use **Service Bus Explorer,** an open source project which you can download from the following link:

https://github.com/paolosalvatori/ServiceBusExplorer/releases

This is a tool which helps us to send a message to the queue rather than going on Azure Portal or Creating a separate client to send a message to a queue for our testing purpose and has various other features. You can download or clone this project, and run the executable exe of the project. If you want to learn more about this project, you can visit on the following URL:

https://blogs.msdn.microsoft.com/paolos/2015/03/02/service-bus-explorer-2-6-now-available/ In order to start building a Service Bus Web Job we need a Service Bus, so let's create a Service Bus resource on Azure.

Creating a Service Bus Resource on Azure

1. Go to Azure Portal and Login into the portal.

2. Go to our created Resource group and add a new resource Service Bus as shown in the following screenshot:

Figure 89 Searching a Service bus resource on Azure

3. Click on **Create**.
4. Enter the resource details.

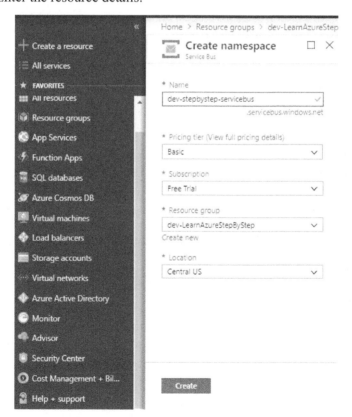

Figure 90 Configuring Service bus resource on Azure

5. Click on the **Create** button. Your service bus resource will be created.

6. Go to your resource group and click on the newly created service bus

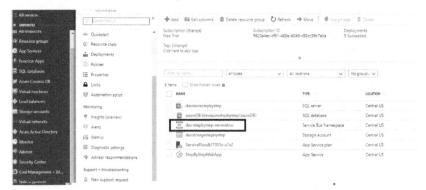

Figure 91 Successfully created Service Bus resource on Azure

7. Copy Connection string from below mentioned figure from service bus shared access policies option and follow the steps:

Figure 92 Extracting Service connection key from Azure

Connecting to service using Service Bus Explorer:

1. Run **ServiceBusExplorer**.

2. If not downloaded yet, download from GitHub as discussed above.

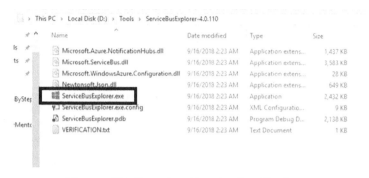

Figure 93 Running ServiceBusExplorer

Figure 94 User Interface of ServiceBusExplorer

3. Click on **File ➤ Connect**.

4. Select **Connection String** in the dropdown as shown in the following figure:

Figure 95 Connecting to Service bus using connection string

Enter your Service bus Connection string which we extracted from shared access policies section.

Figure 96 Entering our Service Bus connection string

5. Click OK and you will see the following options available when we successfully connect to our service bus.

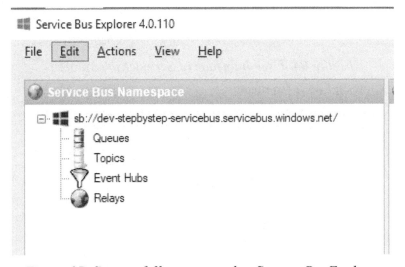

Figure 97 Successfully connected to ServuceBusExplorer

6. For now, we will manually create our queue using service bus explorer which is not a good practice. In QA, UAT and Production

environment, this is not a recommended approach. Usually, in our project, we create a kind of pattern which automatically creates the Queue when the web job is deployed so that we can be assured that we don't have to do this manually.

7. Right Click on **Queues**.

Figure 98 Creating a Queue from ServuceBusExplorer

And name it as per your User Understandability. I will name it as **dbcount**.

Figure 99 Naming a Queue from ServuceBusExplorer

Click **OK**. As soon as you click okay, you will see that a queue has been created, named **dbcount**.

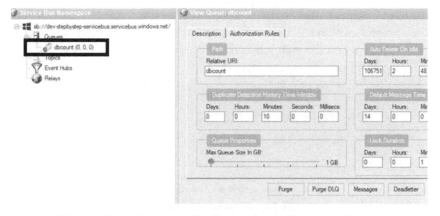

Figure 100 Successfully created our dbcount Queue

The queue can accept messages of the following type:

- XML
- JSON
- String

What I have been doing is to send a message in the form of a string and serializing the message to my class type which we will cover next.

We can do a lot of operations using Service bus Explorer. We majorly perform sending messages, reading messages, purging the queue to delete all messages from queue, and so on.

Now let's make things more realistic, take a real-life requirement to make this example more realistic and helpful to all. How about creating a Service Trigger web job which sends mail to the received emailed from the queue message. I believe that in every web application sending email is a basic requirement. What we can do is create one more queue named **emailsend** queue by doing the above steps once again.

Once you are done with the homework your queues will look like the following screenshot:

Figure 101 Figure showing emailsend queue

Let's talk about sending email in the normal on premises server. We usually have SMTP server that we use to send email from a registered email ID. On Azure, we can use **SendGrid** service to send emails to our users by sending them tabular reports, sending admin registered user reports, reset password link to users etc. In order to use the **SendGrid** service we need to a **SendGrid** account.

Setting up Send Grid Resource on Azure

So now let's create a Send Grid account on Azure step by step:

1. Go to the resource group.

2. Add a new resource.

3. Search for **SendGrid** Email Delivery.

Figure 102 Searching Send Grid Email Delivery Resource

4. Select **SendGrid** service and create a resource.

5. Select free tier to use free service and configure your credentials for **SendGrid** as shown in the following screenshot:

Figure 103 Showing Send Grid price tier

6. Enter your contact information and agree to Legal terms to get started and then click on **Create**.

7. **SendGrid** to provide us with various features as of now, I will just send a sample mail using a sample template and explain you how we can send dynamic values to **SendGrid** template and then email to customer.

8. Go to your **SendGrid** account from resource group, select send grid.

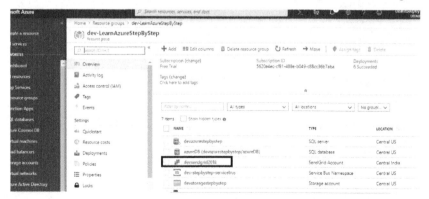

Figure 104 Successfully created SendGrid Account on Azure

9. By default **SendGrid** allows 25000 emails to be sent in free tier. If you want to use more for your production environment you have to buy another service plan.

10. Go to manage option to configure email template in **SendGrid**.

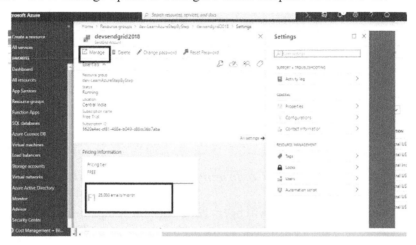

Figure 105 Configuring Send Grid Account

11. A new tab will get open where you will get your **SendGrid** dashboard where you can click and create your template. Check the history how much emails are being sent, how many have unsubscribed from your **SendGrid** emails etc.

Figure 106 Sending confirmation mail to verify
Send Grid Account

12. Confirm your email by logging in to office 365.
13. URL: https://www.office.com/ or directly to outlook and sign in using your credentials.

Figure 107 Confirming Send Grid Account

The **SendGrid** dashboard will open. Now click on Templates and click on Transactional. In order to get started with **SendGrid** in details, you can follow below URL.

https://sendgrid.com/docs

For Templates:

https://sendgrid.com/solutions/email-marketing-templates/

Generate your API Key:

Go to dashboard, then settings select API key menu and click on **Create API Key**.

Figure 108 Generating your Send Grid key

Figure 109 Creating your full access Send Grid key

Click on **Create** and **View**. Copy your **SendGrid** safely to be used in your project.

Figure 110 Successfully retrieved the SendGrid key

Once done, go to your Azure resource and again go to **SendGrid** and manage dashboard and then create your template for email.

Creating Dynamic Template in SendGrid

We can select a design editor to create a template for us or code editor as well to write the HTML for us.

Figure 111 Creating your first dynamic template in Send Grid

Click on **Save** and add version to it and select **Code Editor** option as shown in the following screenshot:

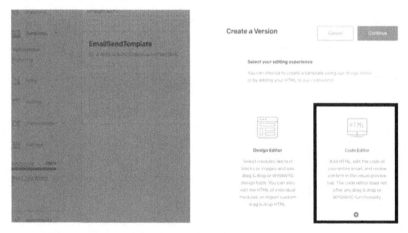

Figure 112 Selecting code editor to edit the template

Click on **Continue**.

Enter your HTML code as per your requirement which should come in email of customers. In our requirement, I will send all registered user list from the DB in the mail and dynamic subject line.

You can check some open source template for the testing purpose from the following links:

https://github.com/sendgrid/email-templates

I have created my template and it looks like the following screenshot:

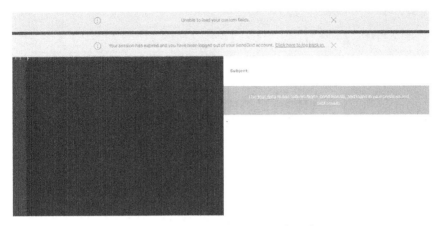

Figure 113 Overview of code editor

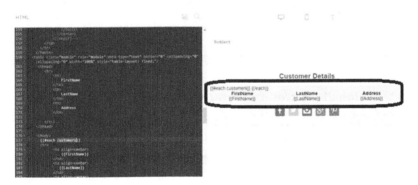

Figure 114 Editing your dynamic template on Send Grid account

We will be showing all user details in the mail.

Let's start writing our Service Bus Trigger Code now and use send grid inside that step by step.

Creating Service Bus Web Job

1. Create a Web Job Project.

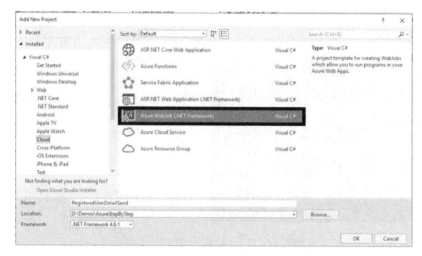

Figure 115 Selecting Azure WebJob Project template

2. I will be using Entity framework to fetch customer details from the database. Install Entity Framework core package from nuget package manager.

3. Also, install **Microsoft.Azure.WebJobs.ServiceBus** for running Web Job on Service Bus Trigger.

4. Install **SendGrid** package to send an email via **SendGrid**.

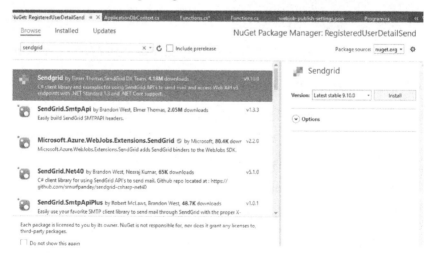

Figure 116 Installing SendGrid nuget package

Copy the Template ID from Send Grid account of template, we just created before, as shown in below figure and Save in **app.config** also add an **AzureWebJobsServiceBus** connection string in **app.config**.

Figure 117 Copying the template id to be used in the Web job

Accessing service bus connection string from the Azure portal.

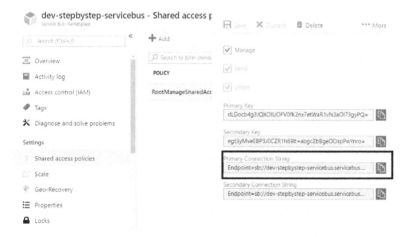

Figure 118 Extracting Service Bus connection string

- As we are using service bus trigger in the **program.cs** file, we need to tell **JobHostConfiguration** that we are using **ServiceBus**.

```
0 references | 0 changes | 0 authors, 0 changes
class Program
{
    // Please set the following connection strings in app.config for this WebJob to run:
    // AzureWebJobsDashboard and AzureWebJobsStorage
    0 references | 0 changes | 0 authors, 0 changes | 0 exceptions
    static void Main()
    {
        var config = new JobHostConfiguration();
        config.UseServiceBus();
        var host = new JobHost(config);
        // The following code ensures that the WebJob will be running continuously
        host.RunAndBlock();
    }
}
```

Figure 119 Configuration to UseServiceBus

Looking at function code:

```
0 references | 0 changes | 0 authors, 0 changes | 0 exceptions
public async static Task ProcessQueueMessage([ServiceBusTrigger("emailsend")] string message, TextWriter log)
{
      Console.WriteLine("The Email Sending Job Starts ");
      // var emailAddress = message;
        var optionsBuilder = new DbContextOptionsBuilder<ApplicationDbContext>();
        optionsBuilder.UseSqlServer(ConfigurationManager.AppSettings["DBConnectionString"]);
        ApplicationDbContext _context = new ApplicationDbContext(optionsBuilder.Options);
        List<Customer> customers = _context.Customers.ToList();
    //writting code in this context only this should be in separate reusable library
    var apiKey = ConfigurationManager.AppSettings["SENDGRID_API_KEY"];
    var templateId = ConfigurationManager.AppSettings["TEMPLATEID"];
    var client = new SendGridClient(apiKey);
    var from = new EmailAddress("LearnStepByStep12@outlook.com","LearnAzure");
    EmailAddress emailAddress = new EmailAddress(message,message);
    var msg = new SendGridMessage()
    {
        From = from,
        Subject = "Azure step by step",
        TemplateId= templateId
    };
    Dictionary<string, List<Customer>> customerDic = new Dictionary<string, List<Customer>>();
    customerDic.Add("customers", customers);
    msg.Personalizations = new List<Personalization>();
    msg.Personalizations.Add(new Personalization()
    {
        TemplateData = customerDic
    });

    msg.AddTo(emailAddress);
    var response = await client.SendEmailAsync(msg);
  }
}
```

Figure 120 Code to send mail

For now, I have written all code in a single file only. This responsibility should be given to other helper, Repository, or Service class.

You can clearly see I am using my send Grid API key, **TemplateId** and retrieving all customer details from DB and passing to send grid.

Once you are done writing the code you can run the project.

Figure 121 Running the Service Bus triggered Web Job

We can see the message that **ServicePointManager**. **DefaultConnectionLimit** is set to 2, which is used to control the number of concurrent connections to a specific host.

In order to run the service bus trigger web job, let's send a genuine email message into the **emailsend** queue as shown in the following figure:

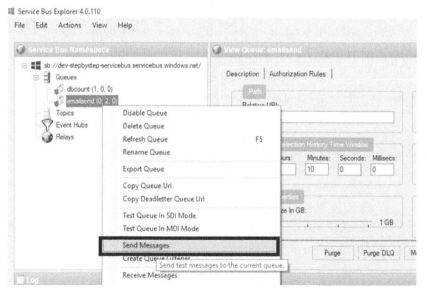

Figure 122 Initiating to send message into the queue

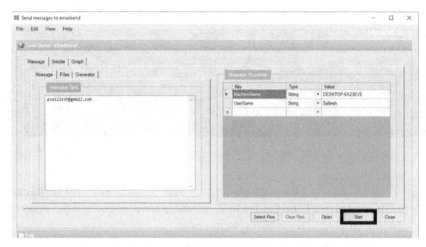

Figure 123 Sending message into the queue

As our web job accepts an email address, I am sending my email address to be used and will send my website registered user's details on mail.

As soon as you send a message on to the queue the job will get triggered.

Figure 124 Breakpoint gets hit as soon as message is send to queue

This will then send an email with registered customer detail to email ID which passed in the message.

Figure 125 Customer details email received from Send Grid

You can see the email received from the **SendGrid**.

Deploying Service Bus trigger Web Job on Azure: Let's
deploy the Web Job on Azure. We will use the same step that we followed
for Timer Trigger job but this time set run mode as **Run Continuously**.

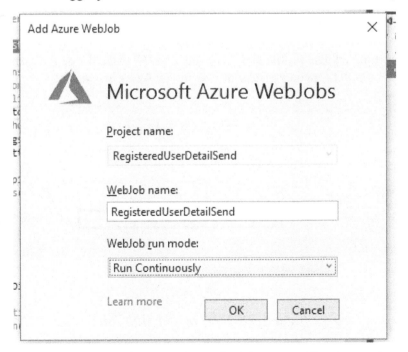

Figure 126 Configuring the Web Job as Run Continuously

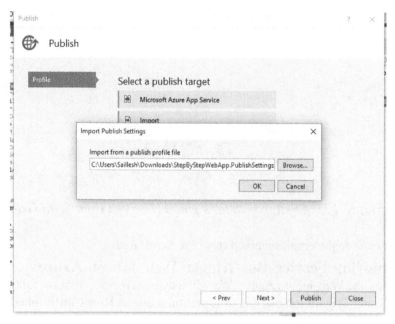

Figure 127 Importing Publish profile Web job

Import the publish profile and then click on **OK**. Once the deployment is successful, let's go and check our web job on Azure and start it.

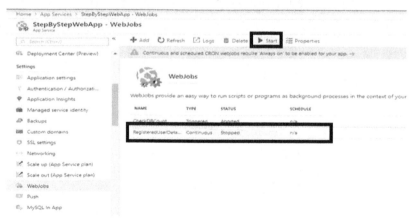

Figure 128 Starting our Web Job

Once the Web Job is deployed, before running your web job set *Always On* the configuration as on.

Always On setting on Azure web app increases application responsiveness, especially if the application is not very frequently accessed by users. For continues job to be in running mode despite our web app being idle enable *Always On*.

In case your Web Job is not running despite clicking on start many times, check logs section and see if you are facing an error script *dotnet-aspnet-codegenerator-design.exe* with script host - *WindowsScriptHost* remove *Microsoft.VisualStudio.Web.CodeGeneration* from the *csproj* file.

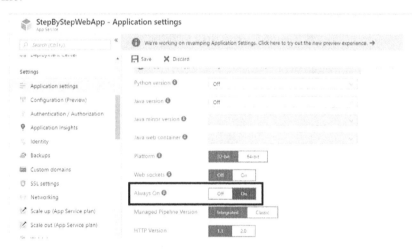

Figure 129 Enabling Always on feature

Figure 130 Web Job starts running

Click on **Logs**.

Now send a message to the queue using service explorer and check the logs to check if the job is working as per our expectations or not?

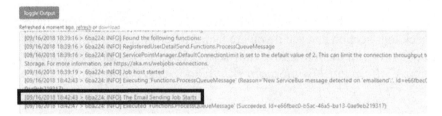

Figure 131 Web Job generated logs

Congrats, your first Service bus trigger job is running successfully. Check your email for an email received from **SendGrid**.

Figure 132 Email received from deployed Web job

So in this Chapter, you have learned all about Timer Trigger and Service Bus Triggered jobs.

Day 6: Creating Your First Cloud Service App on Azure

Before diving in this chapter, we will be discussing the Cloud service PAAS and creating and deploying our cloud service and real-life example of worker role on Azure. We will look into benefits of using Cloud Service as compared to Web App.

Cloud Service was the first service which was provided by Microsoft in PaaS offering. It is an old classic way of deploying web and background service on Azure, broadly known as old Deployment model on Azure. Azure handles all the initialization of the servers, deployment and windows update which we will see in the chapter. Cloud Service and Web App differ in various and extensibility in features. In web app we easily and quickly were able to start and deploy the jobs and web application, extendibility was easy, and we were just focusing on our web app without having control of the environment.

In cloud service, we have full rights (full control) to install any software on server. We can log into actual machine via Remote desktop Protocol and check the server, access the registry and most important the sandbox restrictions are not forced in Azure Cloud Service. The number of web role and worker role we deploy is same of as the number of instances of VM are to be created. If we scale up the web/worker role the number of instance of VM are increased. You can do all kinds of diagnostics adding performance counter of your app.

With full control access you lose some speed as compared to Web App. The major disadvantage. I personally find on cloud service was time-consuming deployment process. Even for scaling a worker role it takes minutes whereas in Web App it's quick. The number of instance count is present in configuration and you need to redeploy the app to change it.

Creating Your First Cloud Service

Let's start and create our first Cloud Service using Visual Studio. Our Cloud Service will consist of one Web Role same application which we did in web app and one worker role with same Publisher and Subscriber pattern which will get triggered when message is sent to the queue. In order to make it real life example, I will create a Worker Role job which take snapshot of our web app using **phantom.js** and will verify that we are able to use Graphics API which were restricted in Web App. I will be adding a new project to my existing solution which we did in the previous chapters.

1. Open Visual Studio.
2. Add new Project.
3. Select Azure Cloud Service.

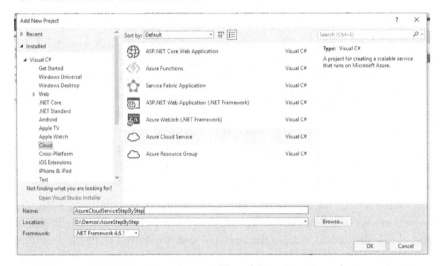

Figure 133 Selecting Azure Cloud Service Template project

4. Select one Web Role and one Service Bus trigger Worker Role as shown in the following screenshot:

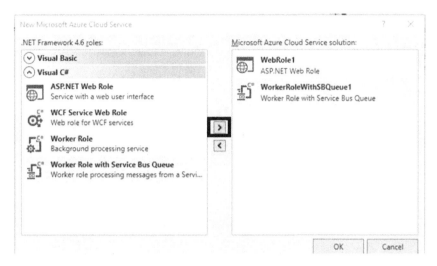

Figure 134 Selecting the Web and Worker role from services provide by Cloud Service

5. Click on edit to rename your project as shown in following screenshot:

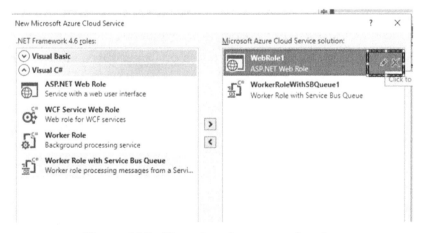

Figure 135 Changing the name of project

Figure 136 Project name changed successfully

6. Click on **OK**.

7. Select framework to be used for Web App. (Note: By default, Cloud service doesn't allow ASP.NET Core app). In case you want to do that, you can follow the following article to do it. https://oren.codes/2017/10/16/using-asp-net-core-with-azure-cloud-services/

8. Select MVC as of now, to create a project and then click on **OK** button.

Figure 137 Selecting MVC template

9. Once visual studio is done creating project, you will see the following project structure:

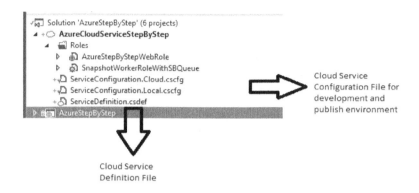

Figure 138 Defining cscfg and csdef

Understanding the configuration file in Cloud Service:

1. **Cloud Service Configuration File (CSCFG):** This file contains the configuration used by the web and web role as shown in the following screenshot:

```
ServiceConfiguration.Cloud.cscfg  ⊣  ⊅  ✕  WorkerRole.cs      AzureStepByStepWebRole      appsettings.json      Team Explorer - Connect      App.config      Program.cs
 1    <?xml version="1.0" encoding="utf-8"?>
 2    <ServiceConfiguration serviceName="AzureCloudServiceStepByStep" xmlns="http://schemas.microsoft.com/ServiceHosting/2008/10/ServiceConfiguration" o
 3      <Role name="AzureStepByStepWebRole">
 4        <Instances count="1" />
 5        <ConfigurationSettings>
 6          <Setting name="Microsoft.WindowsAzure.Plugins.Diagnostics.ConnectionString" value="UseDevelopmentStorage=true" />
 7        </ConfigurationSettings>
 8      </Role>
 9      <Role name="SnapshotWorkerRoleWithSBQueue">
10        <Instances count="1" />
11        <ConfigurationSettings>
12          <Setting name="Microsoft.WindowsAzure.Plugins.Diagnostics.ConnectionString" value="UseDevelopmentStorage=true" />
13          <Setting name="Microsoft.ServiceBus.ConnectionString" value="Endpoint=sb://[your namespace].servicebus.windows.net;SharedAccessKeyName=RootM
14        </ConfigurationSettings>
15      </Role>
16    </ServiceConfiguration>
```

Figure 139 Cloud Service configuration file

- It contains information like Number of instance to be allocated to our Web Role and Worker Role.
- Diagnostics should be enabled or not?
- Connection string for service.

You can change these configuration manually as per your requirement or you can use graphical interface by right clicking on Web or Worker Role file on Cloud Service Solution as shown in the following screenshot and configure your environment.

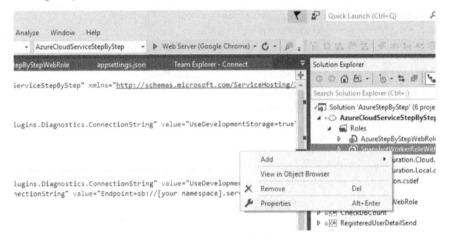

Figure 140 Changing configuration from User Interface

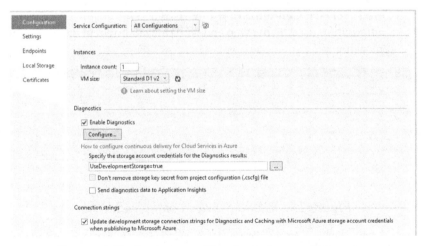

Figure 141 Setting up Cloud service configuration

You can configure the Diagnostics and add more performance counter and other logs to be included for your environment. As you can see all these will be provided to you when you deploy your Cloud Service. Normally in on-premises VM we have to do all this manually: raising a ticket first for configuring the server like Installing IIS, virtual networks, Drives etc. which usually takes 1-2 days varying business to business. But over here all this will be provided by Microsoft Azure. We simply have to just think to solve the customer business problem and Microsoft will handle all configuration part for us.

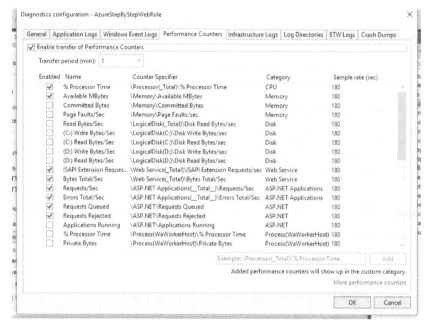

Figure 142 Enabling Performance Counter

2. In the Web Role part, I will be just showing the customer details which we did in our Web App project to fasten the process. As this is an ASP.NET MVC app I will be using Entity Framework to connect our DB. If you want to get started with Entity Framework you can read my basic article from below link:

   https://www.c-sharpcorner.com/UploadFile/cb1429/getting-started-with-entity-framework/

3. You can see the entire code in the GitHub repository to see what is actually been done.

4. Once you are done setting up the connection with DB run your web app on your local machine. You will be able to see same records as we saw in Web app chapter.

Figure 143 Customer List User Interface

So we are ready to deploy our Cloud Service Project. But in Cloud Service, we can't deploy Web Role and Worker Role separately as they are part of same cloud service project. So now we will continue with the development of our Worker Role now, and once we are done with Worker Role development we will deploy them together.

Creating Your First Worker Role with Service Bus Trigger

As of now as we discussed we will be creating a job which will take snapshot of our customer page and send it on email using send grid. This is real life use case which you can get in your respective project requirement.

Let's go through the worker role project structure first.

Application Start:

```
public override bool OnStart()
{
    // Set the maximum number of concurrent connections
    ServicePointManager.DefaultConnectionLimit = 12;

    // Create the queue if it does not exist already
    string connectionString = CloudConfigurationManager.GetSetting("Microsoft.ServiceBus.Conn
    var namespaceManager = NamespaceManager.CreateFromConnectionString(connectionString);
    if (!namespaceManager.QueueExists(QueueName))
    {
        namespaceManager.CreateQueue(QueueName);
    }

    // Initialize the connection to Service Bus Queue
    Client = QueueClient.CreateFromConnectionString(connectionString, QueueName);
    return base.OnStart();
}

public override void OnStop()
{
    // Close the connection to Service Bus Queue
    Client.Close();
    CompletedEvent.Set();
    base.OnStop();
}
```

Figure 144 Project structure of Worker Role

Whenever our worker role starts or loads it will first run **OnStart()** function where it get all the details just like **Program.cs** file in Web Jobs. This code as mentioned in comment section loads the configuration setting from app setting or **CloudConfigurationManager** and run the Worker Role.

Variables

const string QueueName = "ProcessingQueue";

This is queue name from where by default, worker role will read messages or subscribed to messages. We will change the name as per our Task.

On Message arrival:

```
public override void Run()
{
    Trace.WriteLine("Starting processing of messages");

    // Initiates the message pump and callback is invoked for each message that is received, calling close on the client will stop the pump.
    Client.OnMessage((receivedMessage) =>
    {
        try
        {
            // Process the message
            Trace.WriteLine("Processing Service Bus message: " + receivedMessage.SequenceNumber.ToString());
        }
        catch
        {
            // Handle any message processing specific exceptions here
        }
    });

    CompletedEvent.WaitOne();
}
```

Figure 145 Code execution when message comes into the queue

When the message comes in queue the Run method gets executed and executes our logic. The worker role also have service configuration where you can mention the number of instances of VM, diagnostics etc.

Figure 146 Worker role configuration

You can set the service bus connection string setting section of configuration as shown in the following screenshot:

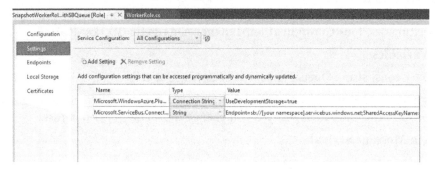

Figure 147 Using the connection string

As our worker role is service bus triggered we need to create a queue which will trigger this worker role. I will follow the same steps we followed in before chapter using Service Bus Explorer to send message to the queue.

Figure 148 Creating a new Queue named snapshotqueue

We have named the queue name as **"snapshotqueue"**.

Taking Snapshot using PhantomJs

So now in order to take a snapshot of web application or web page I will be using **Phantom.js**. I will be using **NReco.PhantomJS** nuget package.

You can read the documentation from the following URL in case you want to use this package:

https://www.nrecosite.com/phantomjs_wrapper_net.aspx

http://phantomjs.org/

http://phantomjs.org/api/webpage/method/render-base64.html

Install **NReco.PhantomJS** from Nuget package manager and also install send grid for sending email.

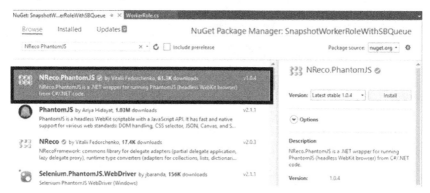

Figure 149 Installing NReco nuget package

Phantom JS help us take snapshot of Web Application which is Web Browser which exists in scripts, so in order to achieve the same we will have to create a new JavaScript file.

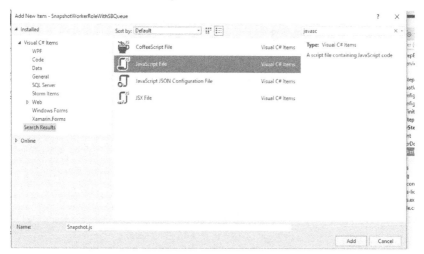

Figure 150 Adding a JavaScript file for NReco

Before writing any code, let's create a sample send grid template to be sent on email:

Figure 151 Creating Send Grid template for emailing snapshot

So our basic template will show Heading as Website Snapshot and will have image down in middle.

Write the following code in the **Snapshot.js** file.

```
SnapshotWorkerRoleWithSBQueue JavaScript Content Files        ▾  ⊕  <function>
 1    var webPage = require('webpage');
 2    system = require('system')
 3    var page = webPage.create();
 4    phantom.onError = function (ex) {
 5        console.log(ex);
 6        phantom.exit();
 7    }
 8    page.viewportSize = {
 9        width: 1920,
10        height: 1080
11    };
12    var address = system.args[1];
13    //console.log(address);
14    page.open(address, function (status) {
15        try {
16            var base64 = page.renderBase64('PNG');
17          console.log(base64);
18            phantom.exit();
19        }
20        catch (ex) {
21            console.log(console.log(ex));
22            phantom.exit();
23        }
24    });
25
26
27
```

Figure 152 JavaScript code that gets executed by Phantom.js

Code File:

```
var base64Image = string.Empty;
//this code should be in library of Phatom
var snapshotFilePath = Path.Combine(AppDomain.CurrentDomain.BaseDirectory, "Snapshot.js");
var phantomJS = new PhantomJS();
phantomJS.OutputReceived += (sender, e) => {
    if (!string.IsNullOrEmpty(e.Data))
    {
        base64Image = e.Data;
    }
};
phantomJS.ErrorReceived += (sender, e) => {
    throw new Exception(e.Data);
};
var url= ConfigurationManager.AppSettings["applicationUrl"];
//var scriptText = File.ReadAllText(snapshotFilePath);
// phantomJS.RunScript(scriptText, null);
phantomJS.Run(snapshotFilePath,new string[] { url });

//send grid code should be separate library
var apiKey = ConfigurationManager.AppSettings["SENDGRID_API_KEY"];
var templateId = ConfigurationManager.AppSettings["TEMPLATEID"];
var client = new SendGridClient(apiKey);
var from = new EmailAddress("LearnStepByStep12@outlook.com", "LearnAzure");
EmailAddress emailAddress = new EmailAddress("psaillesh@gmail.com","Saillesh Pawar");
var msg = new SendGridMessage()
{
    From = from,
    Subject = "Azure step by step",
    TemplateId = templateId
};

msg.AddTo(emailAddress);
msg.AddAttachment("SnapshotImage", base64Image, "image/jpg", "inline", "Snapshotimage");
var status=   client.SendEmailAsync(msg).Result;
```

Figure 153 Code to take snapshot from phantom.js and send bas64 on email

Let us run both project simultaneously. In case you don't know how to run two projects simultaneously in Visual studio just click on properties on Project Solution as shown in the following screenshot:

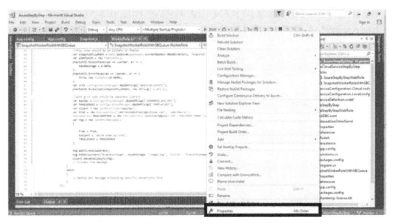

Figure 154 Configuring Visual studio to run two projects

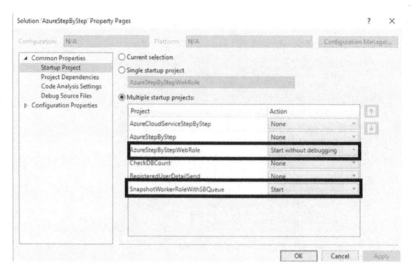

Figure 155 Selecting project to be started parallel

Once done let's debug our worker role in order to check if everything is working fine or not? Make sure before debugging send message to the queue that we just created in order to trigger worker role. In our worker role, there is no message type restriction to run the job. Any message will be considered as triggering snapshot worker role.

You will get a running worker role, with multiple projects. While debugging this project I learned something new and want to share with you.

- As we have our web app and cloud service project in single solution. So when I was trying to run only worker role it was not allowing me to run and showed this error:

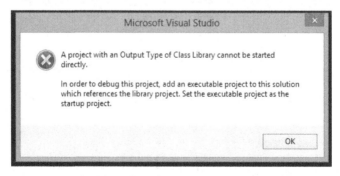

Figure 156 Error while running worker role

I learned that in order to run worker role I have to set my cloud service project as startup project, not worker role project.

- Another learning I want to share while working in my organization where I didn't had administrative access, I was not able to run worker role. So you need to run Visual Studio as administrator so that Visual Studio can run azure emulator on local machine to debug the same.

- There will be many times, when you will get an error stating "cannot access cxf folder", try to clean the project and run.

Figure 157 Clean the project to solve this issue

Run the project and check whether everything is working fine or not?

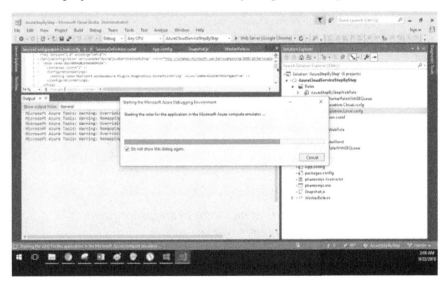

Figure 158 Starting Azure emulator to run worker role on local machine

As soon as emulator start, your worker role **OnStart()** function will get executed as shown in the following screenshot:

```
SnapshotWorkerRoleWithSBQueue                              ▾  SnapshotWorkerRoleWithSBQueue.WorkerRole          ▾  ⚙ OnStart()
79          CompletedEvent.WaitOne();
80      }
81
82      public override bool OnStart()
83      {
84          // Set the maximum number of concurrent connections
85          ServicePointManager.DefaultConnectionLimit = 12;
86
87          // Create the queue if it does not exist already
88          string connectionString = CloudConfigurationManager.GetSetting("Microsoft.ServiceBus.ConnectionString");
89          var namespaceManager = NamespaceManager.CreateFromConnectionString(connectionString);
90          if (!namespaceManager.QueueExists(QueueName))
91          {
92              namespaceManager.CreateQueue(QueueName);
93          }
94
95          // Initialize the connection to Service Bus Queue
96          Client = QueueClient.CreateFromConnectionString(connectionString, QueueName);
97          return base.OnStart();
98      }
99
100     public override void OnStop()
101     {
102         // Close the connection to Service Bus Queue
103         Client.Close();
```

Figure 159 Running of Worker Role on local

Send a sample message to the Queue, as shown in the following screenshot:

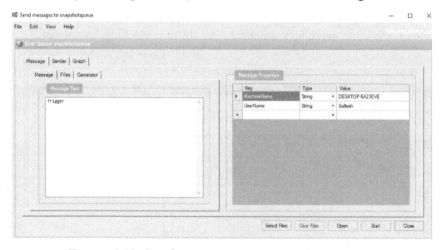

*Figure 160 Sending message to snapshotqueue to
trigger worker role*

This will trigger the worker role now.

Figure 161 Breakpoint hitting as soon as message is received by queue

Check whether the base64 string is correct or not. Go to the website http:// beautifytools.com/base64-to-image-converter.php

Copy and paste the base64 and generate image. You will get the following image:

Figure 162 Checking base 64 string returned by phantom.js

Check your mail, you should have received the following mail similarly as shown in the following screenshot:

Figure 163 Email received from Send grid of Customer list snapshot

Deploying Cloud Service:

Deploying Cloud service is quite easy, you can deploy the cloud service using visual studio if you have admin credentials (**Note**: If you log in to visual studio as admin email, or connect to subscription via admin). You can easily publish the cloud service. Another way is uploading a package file. We will go through each of them step by step.

Deploying via Visual Studio:

When we deploy application or publish application the **Service. Configuration.Cloud** is included for deployment, not **Service. Configuration** .Local as we are publishing the application now on cloud.

Figure 164 Service.Configuration.Cloud.cscfg file being referenced when deploying on Azure

Step 1: Right click on cloud project and click on **Publish**.

Figure 165 Publishing Cloud Service from Visual Studio

Step 2: Add your account to it.

Figure 166 Adding your Azure account to publish Cloud Service

Step 3: Enter your subscription email ID.

Figure 167 Login into visual studio with your Azure credentials

Step 4: Enter password and sign in.

Figure 168 Enter Azure password for adding Azure account

Step 5: Select your subscription and click on **Next**.

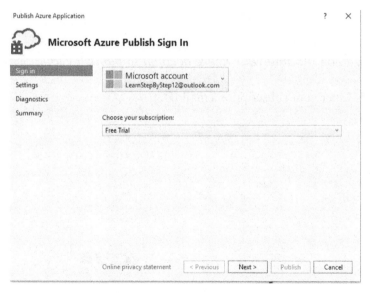

Figure 169 Successfully imported Subscription in Visual Studio

Step 6: Create a cloud Service Resource as we do it in Azure portal and click on **Create**.

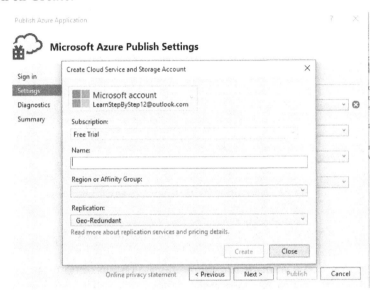

Figure 170 Naming the Cloud Service

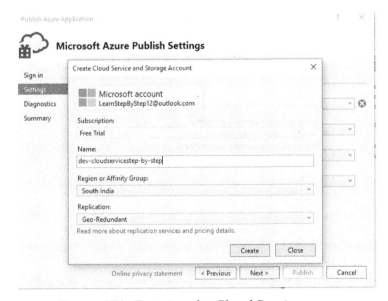

Figure 171 Entering the Cloud Service name

Error while creating cloud service:

Figure 172 Issue while creating Cloud Service

In case you don't want to use the storage, you can ignore the error or enter it again. Basically, we can also upload or publish cloud service by uploading package on storage and set the storage path and upload the package. We will see this further.

In case you get the same problem set storage account setting in both of the following setting in both web role and worker role configuration file.

Figure 173 Add storage account setting in both the diagnostic file

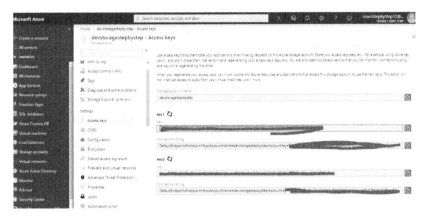

Figure 174 Extracting storage configuration details

Copy Account Name and Key1 and paste in configuration page and save.

```
SnapshotWorkerRol...ithSBQueue [Role]*    diagnostics.wadcfg    diagnostics.wadcfgx*  ⊕ ×
18          <FailedRequestLogs containerName ="wad-failedrequestlogs" />
11          </Directories>
12          <WindowsEventLog scheduledTransferPeriod="PT1M" >
13              <DataSource name="Application![System[(Level=1 or Level=2 or Level=3)]]" />
14              <DataSource name="Windows Azure![System[(Level=1 or Level=3 or Level=4)]]" />
15          </WindowsEventLog>
16          <CrashDumps containerName="wad-crashdumps" dumpType="Mini">
17              <CrashDumpConfiguration processName="waIISHost.exe"/>
18              <CrashDumpConfiguration processName="waworkerHost.exe"/>
19              <CrashDumpConfiguration processName="w3wp.exe"/>
20          </CrashDumps>
21          <PerformanceCounters scheduledTransferPeriod="PT1M">
22              <PerformanceCounterConfiguration counterSpecifier="\Memory\Available MBytes" sampleRate="PT3M" />
23              <PerformanceCounterConfiguration counterSpecifier="\Web Service(_Total)\ISAPI Extension Requests/sec" sampleRate="PT3M" />
24              <PerformanceCounterConfiguration counterSpecifier="\Web Service(_Total)\Bytes Total/Sec" sampleRate="PT3M" />
25              <PerformanceCounterConfiguration counterSpecifier="\ASP.NET Applications(__Total__)\Requests/Sec" sampleRate="PT3M" />
26              <PerformanceCounterConfiguration counterSpecifier="\ASP.NET Applications(__Total__)\Errors Total/Sec" sampleRate="PT3M" />
27              <PerformanceCounterConfiguration counterSpecifier="\ASP.NET\Requests Queued" sampleRate="PT3M" />
28              <PerformanceCounterConfiguration counterSpecifier="\ASP.NET\Requests Rejected" sampleRate="PT3M" />
29              <PerformanceCounterConfiguration counterSpecifier="\Processor(_Total)\% Processor Time" sampleRate="PT3M" />
30          </PerformanceCounters>
31          </DiagnosticMonitorConfiguration>
32      </wadcfg>
33      <StorageAccount></StorageAccount>
34      </PublicConfig>
35      <PrivateConfig>
36          <StorageAccount name="devstoragestepbystep" key="
37              endpoint="core.windows.net" />
38      </PrivateConfig>
39      <IsEnabled>true</IsEnabled>
40  </DiagnosticsConfiguration>
```

Figure 175 Adding Storage configuration that should be used
while deploying Cloud service

Start the publish process again as mentioned above.

Once you are done now common setting page will come as shown in
following screenshot:

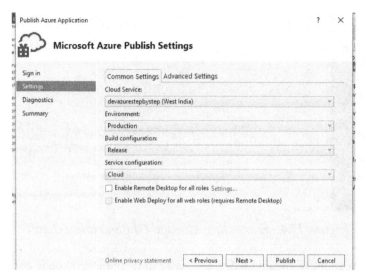

Figure 176 Cloud Service configuration page

We can enable the Remote Desktop protocol in our cloud service as mentioned in the above figure. Just check the Enable Remote Desktop option and set your RDP password.

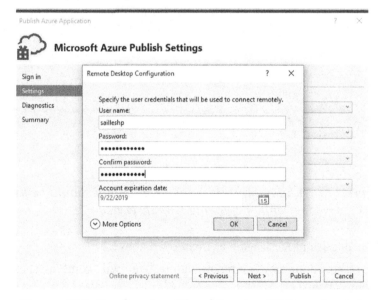

Figure 177 Configuring Cloud Service RDP credentials

Click on **OK**.

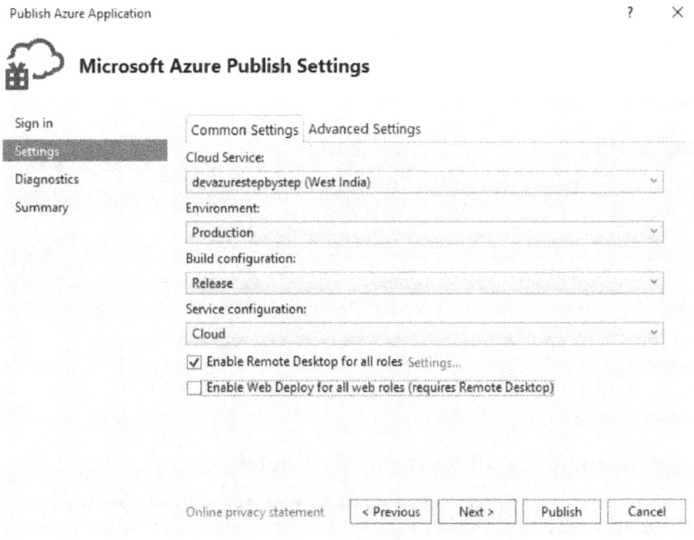

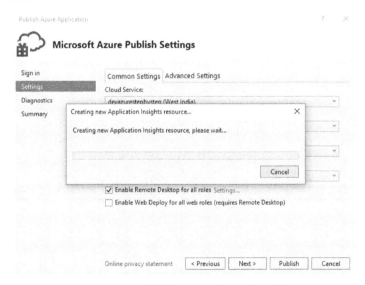

Figure 178 Successfully configured our Cloud Service

Click on **Publish**, you will get a progress bar as shown in the following screenshot:

Figure 179 Publish starts for Cloud Service

Once this is done, our deployment process will start via visual studio. This usually takes minutes to deploy and that is the saddest part because there are lots of configuration and instances that are needed to be created. Microsoft Azure set platform for us that is why it takes time.

Deployment Status

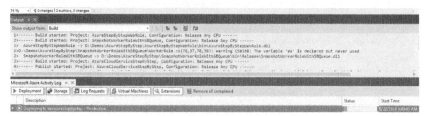

Figure 180 Cloud Service Deployment status

Deployment completed after couple of minutes.

Figure 181 Cloud Service Deployment completed successfully

Now we got Azure portal and look for cloud service in our resources.

Figure 182 Cloud Service resource created on Azure

Click on cloud service, you will see 1 instance of Web and Worker role running.

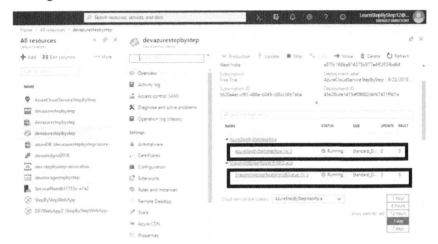

Figure 183 Instances running of Web and Worker role on Azure

We can access our Web role from URL as mentioned in the following screenshot:

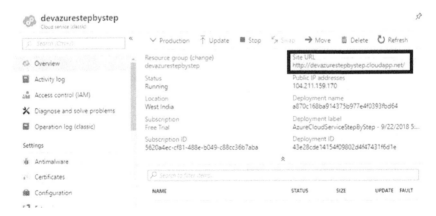

Figure 184 Navigating to Cloud Service Web Role URL

Click on site Url and you can see our Web Role is successfully connected to our DB.

Figure 185 Successfully able to communicate with database

Now let's test our worker role and send a message to the *snapshotqueue* queue.

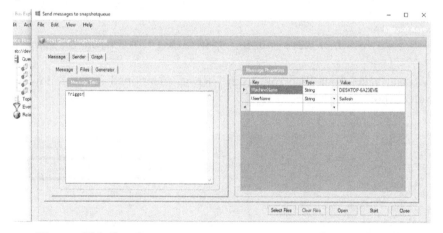

Figure 186 Sending message to queue to invoke Worker role

We have successfully received the snapshot of web application in our email from our Worker Role as shown in the following screenshot:

Let's see where our application is hosted in Cloud Service. As we mentioned Cloud Service Microsoft provides us the platform as a service so IIS configuration and all other stuff will be taken care of by Microsoft. Our application would be hosted by them. Web Role and Worker role will have separate VM.

Figure 187 Email received from SendGrid from Worker role running on Azure

Connect to RDP using Azure Portal Step By Step:

- Click on **Web Role** than click on **Connect**.
- If RDP is not enabled, you can enable the same from Remote desktop options.
- Once you click on **Connect**, RDP file would be downloaded.

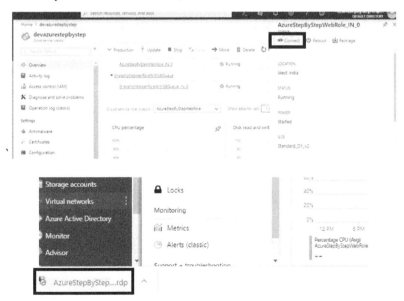

Figure 188 Connecting to Cloud Service Worker Role

Open the RDP file and connect. Enter your RDP password and you are good to go.

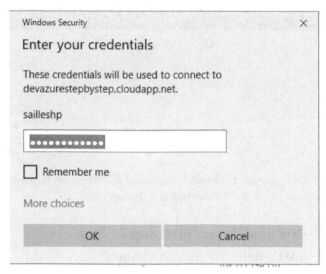

Figure 189 Entering the VM credentials

- Open IIS from server manager

Figure 190 Accessing IIS server to see the Web role

You will see the web role created by you, hosted on IIS as shown in the following screenshot:

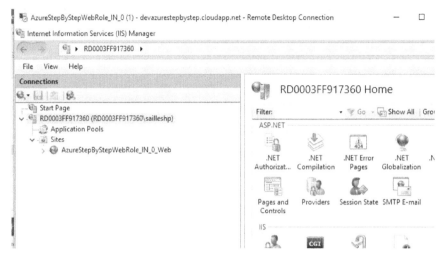

Figure 191 Demonstrating Web role deployed on IIS

Deploying Cloud Service as a Package

We can also deploy the Cloud Service via the package. We will create the package using Visual Studio and then we will upload the package ZIP file on Azure portal. Let's get started.

1. Right click on Cloud Service project and click on **Package**.

Figure 192 Deploying Cloud Service as a Package

2. Select Release mode for Package and then click on **Package**.

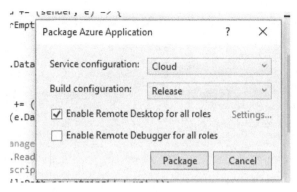

Figure 193 Dialog to Select Package option

3. Once the package is created, the folder containing the package will open with two files.

Figure 194 Cloud Service package Unit

4. The **Cloud Service Package contains our actual code (Cspkg)**

5. The Cscgf **Cloud Service Configuration File (Cscgf)**

6. Now go to Azure portal and click on worker role resource, overview page will open.

Figure 195 Deploying Cloud Service from Azure

You can stop your VM before uploading the file, click on **Update**.

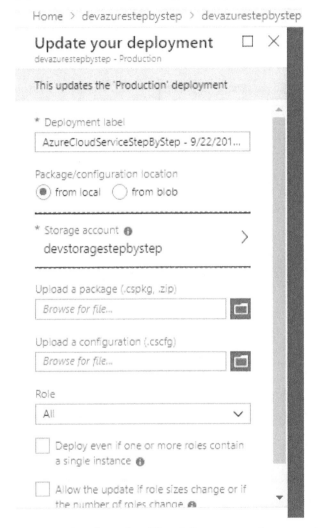

Figure 196 Uploading the Cloud Service package on Azure

Upload the **.cspkg** and **.cscfg** on desired options. You need to select the Storage type because package is uploaded on storage type first and then they are deployed afterward.

Once you upload the file, the uploading will start.

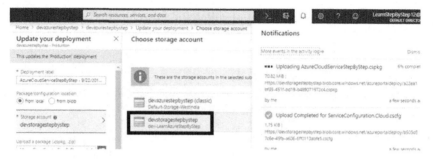

Figure 197 Select Storage account to be used for upload

Once the package has been uploaded, you will see:

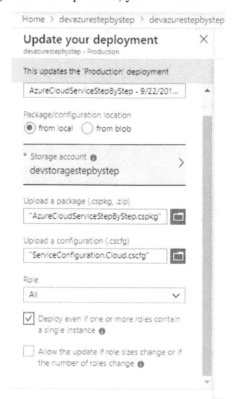

Figure 198 Configuring Cloud Service deployment on Azure

Check deploy, even if one more role contain a single instance because our web role and worker role are single instance right now. Then click on **Ok**.

Once the package is uploaded successfully you can start the VM again.

Figure 199 Successfully deployed Cloud Service from Azure portal

And then go to your website URL and you can check whether your new changes are visible to your website or not.

Index

Create New

FirstName	LastName	Address	
Sailiesh	Pawar	Dehradun	Edit	Details	Delete
Shiv	Prasad	Nepal	Edit	Details	Delete
yogesh	saswade	Dudhwala tower	Edit	Details	Delete

Figure 200 Cloud Service running after deployment

Day 7: Logic/Function as a Service Often Termed as Serverless Computing, Creating Your First Azure Function on Microsoft Azure

Before diving in in this chapter, we will be discussing the Logic as a service PaaS and creating and deploying our Azure function with real-life example and deploy the same on Azure. We will look into the benefits of using Azure function compared with Web Jobs.

Both Azure functions and Logic Apps are termed as serverless application because there is no infrastructure needed to be maintained, auto-scaling and you are billed based on the number of executions. If we have small duration running function, we can run them on consumption plan where we are billed based number of execution. If our jobs are long-running we can run azure function on app service plan as well, which we will be charged daily as per app service plan.

Azure Functions

Azure functions are part of the web app PAAS in order to run our small piece of logic which can be timer triggered, Service Bus triggered e.g.: Storage, Service Bus, Topics etc. They are processing on Top of events (IOT, Event hub etc.), Web API for HTTP triggered Azure functions, communicating between two systems, Publisher, and Subscriber Bus. HTTP bindings for Functions as API, you can create an Azure function from Azure portal itself or using Visual Studio which we are going to use in this chapter. We should use Azure function for short running jobs. We will be creating a new Azure function to solve our previous business problems. You can create Azure function inside azure portal as well and in Visual Studio. In case you want to create complex Azure function, it's well recommended to use visual studio.

Creating Your First Azure Function using Visual Studio

Step 1: Open Visual Studio.

Step 2: Add a new Azure Function project to our existing solution.

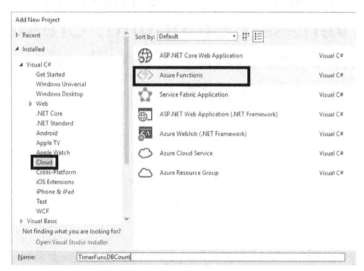

Figure 201 Selecting Azure function template

Microsoft Azure Provides Various Types of Azure Function

Figure 202 Selecting Timer trigger Azure function

We can see in the above diagram, various kinds of Azure function triggers. We have already done Timer Trigger, Service Bus Queue Trigger in our Web Job and Worker Role. But we can also use other Triggers to execute our functions i.e. Blob trigger, Cosmos DB Trigger, Event hub trigger, and HTTP Trigger. In this demo, we will be using timer trigger function.

Step 3: Select Timer Trigger function and then select your storage account:

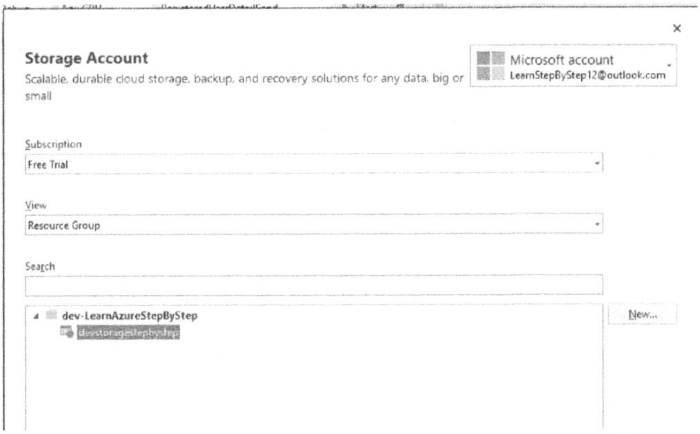

Figure 203 Selecting Storage account to be used in Azure function

As of now we can omit the Schedule part and let's jump to Project structure of Azure function.

Before we use to create Azure function directly on Azure portal so it was difficult to create complex Azure function on Portal but now new Azure Function SDK in Visual Studio we can solve any kind of complex problem.

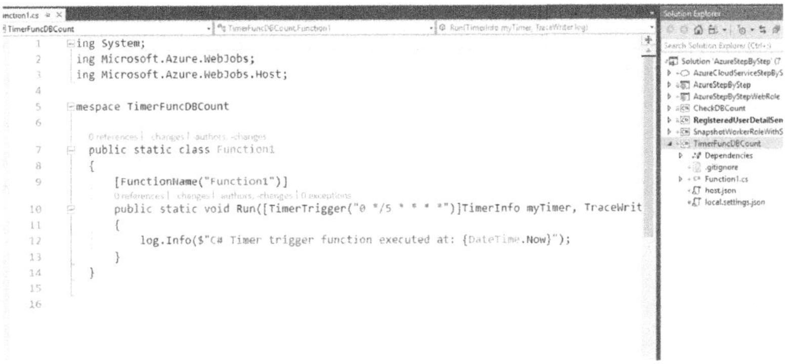

Figure 204 Project structure of Azure function

An Azure function project can consist of multiple Azure functions which can differ in Trigger event i.e. one function can be Timer trigger while other Being Service Trigger etc.

Azure Function is a small piece of function which is just like our small function in C#. We can see it has **Void Run ()** method with other attributes Event Type: Timer Trigger, TraceWriter for logging.

The project has **Local.settings.json** which is typical **app.config** file but in JSON format. In many Azure function I have seen these values coming from Azure key vault because we want our configuration to be secure. In this demo we will store Function configuration in **Local.settings.json** to be used in application.

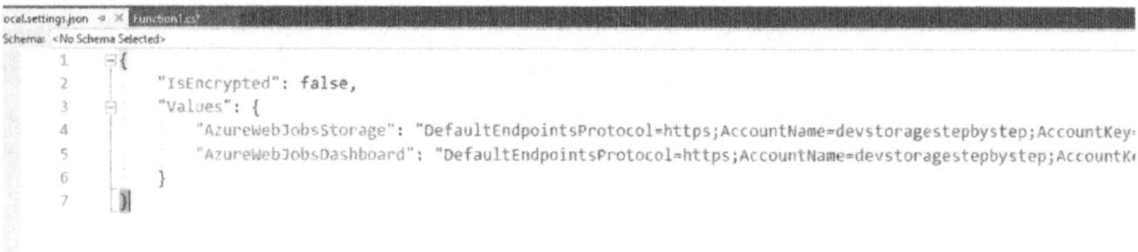

```
ocal.settings.json    Function1.cs
Schema: <No Schema Selected>
  1    {
  2        "IsEncrypted": false,
  3        "Values": {
  4            "AzureWebJobsStorage": "DefaultEndpointsProtocol=https;AccountName=devstoragestepbystep;AccountKey
  5            "AzureWebJobsDashboard": "DefaultEndpointsProtocol=https;AccountName=devstoragestepbystep;AccountKe
  6        }
  7    }
```

Figure 205 Azure function configuration settings

Host.json contains global configuration for all the Azure functions present in our Azure function app for example: Increasing timeout time of Azure function, enabling application insights, Durable tasks to enabled durable functions, lock period timeout.

```
host.json    packages.config    Program.cs    Functions.cs
Schema: http://json.schemastore.org/host
  1    {
  2        "functionTimeout": "00:05:00",
  3        "healthMonitor": {
  4            "enabled": true,
  5            "healthCheckInterval": "00:00:10",
  6            "healthCheckWindow": "00:02:00",
  7            "healthCheckThreshold": 6,
  8            "counterThreshold": 0.80
  9        },
 10        "serviceBus": {
 11            "maxConcurrentCalls": 16,
 12            "prefetchCount": 100,
 13            "autoRenewTimeout": "00:05:00"
 14        }
 15    }
```

Figure 206 Configuring host.json file

In this chapter, we will try to show the number of registered Users in our website after every five minutes, which we solved earlier via using web jobs.

By default Azure function gets timeout in one minute. If you want to increase Azure function timeout, you need to increase timeout in **host. config** file.

I have added the Timer Trigger Schedule of the function in **local.settings. json** file which will be used by Azure function to trigger at that particular schedule as shown in the following screenshot:

```
Function1.cs    local.settings.json  ⊗ ×
Schema: <No Schema Selected>
     1    ⊟{
     2          "IsEncrypted": false,
     3     ⊟    "Values": {
     4            "RunTime": "0 */5 * * * *",
     5          "DBConnectionString": "Data Source=devazurestepbystep.database.windows.net;Initial Catalog=az
     6          "AzureWebJobsStorage": "DefaultEndpointsProtocol=https;AccountName=devstoragestepbystep;Accou
     7          "AzureWebJobsDashboard": "DefaultEndpointsProtocol=https;AccountName=devstoragestepbystep;Acc
     8          }
     9    }
```

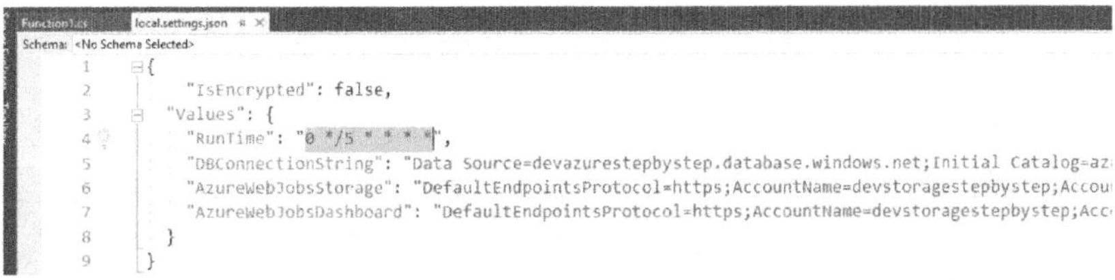

Figure 207 Cron expression added in configuration file

I have also added necessary configuration settings for connecting to DB, storage configuration and web jobs Configurations.

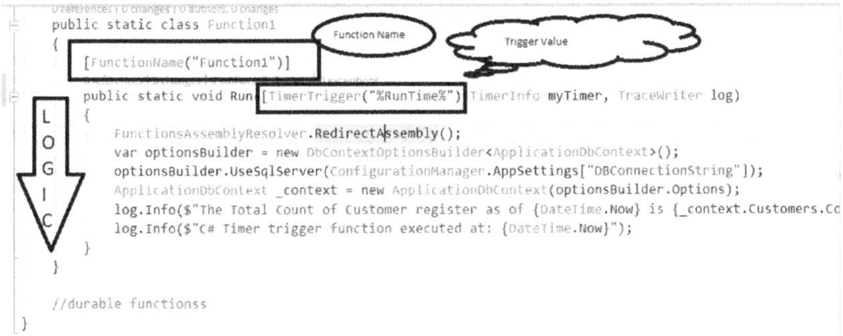

```
0 references | 0 changes | 0 authors, 0 changes
public static class Function1
{
    [FunctionName("Function1")]

    public static void Run([TimerTrigger("%RunTime%")]TimerInfo myTimer, TraceWriter log)
    {
        FunctionsAssemblyResolver.RedirectAssembly();
        var optionsBuilder = new DbContextOptionsBuilder<ApplicationDbContext>();
        optionsBuilder.UseSqlServer(ConfigurationManager.AppSettings["DBConnectionString"]);
        ApplicationDbContext _context = new ApplicationDbContext(optionsBuilder.Options);
        log.Info($"The Total count of customer register as of {DateTime.Now} is {_context.Customers.Cc
        log.Info($"C# Timer trigger function executed at: {DateTime.Now}");
    }
}

//durable functionss
}
```

Function Name

Trigger Value

L O G I C

Figure 208 Understanding Azure Function Run syntax

Once you are done with your code of Azure function you can set the project as startup project and run your azure function, as shown in the following screenshot:

Figure 209 Running Azure function on local machine

The Azure function will start automatically as per the Cron expression set.

Figure 210 Azure function running as per our expectations

Deploying Azure Function to Azure via Visual Studio

Step 1: Right click on your Azure function project as shown in the following screenshot:

Figure 211 Publishing Azure function using Visual Studio

Step 2: Create a new Azure Function App Service.

Figure 212 Create a new Azure App Service for Azure function

If you want to update it next time, and if there is any code change then you can use **Select Existing**. **Select Existing** will replace the old functions with newly uploaded Azure functions.

Click on **Publish:**

Figure 213 Configuring Azure Function Page as you go plan

For hosting plan, we will be using **consumption plan** with Y1 in Hosting plan option which means we will be charged when our Azure functions are running. You can use app service plan as well which will consume your app service resources (web app) that would be used for other cases when your jobs are long-running, you need more resources, etc.

Once you are done configuring the Azure function, click on **Create**.

This step will check for the Function name, whether it exists or not. And then starts' deploying the changes after Function is configured as shown in the following screenshot:

Figure 214 Azure function deployment starts

Once the output window shows publish complete, we can go to Portal and check our Azure function as shown in the following screenshot:

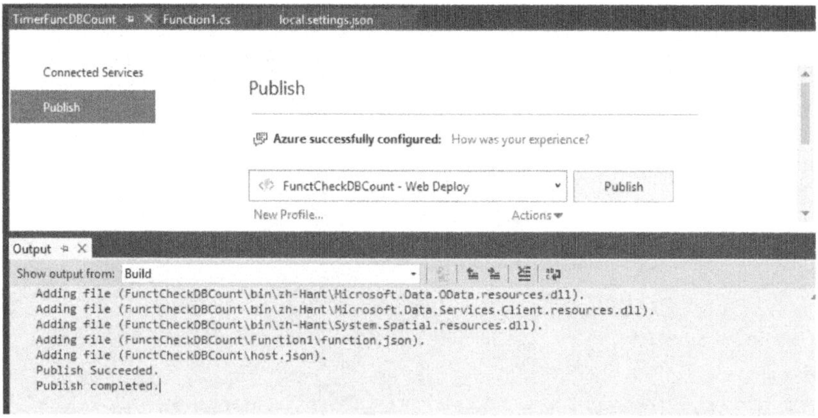

Figure 215 Azure function deployment completed successfully

Figure 216 Azure function successfully deployed on our Resource Group

Save the Configuration

Click on Azure function, we need to add our custom configuration in Application Settings page as shown in the following screenshot:

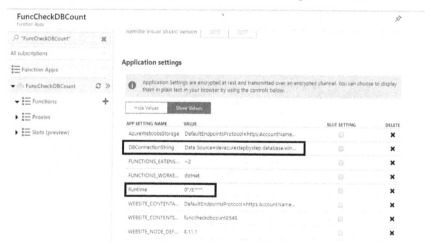

Figure 217 Adding Azure function Application setting on Azure

If you have many application configuration settings, I will suggest you to use https://resources.azure.com and follow the link:

https://stackoverflow.com/questions/49001127/how-to-export-and-import-azure-functions-application-settings

Click on **Function1** and then click on **Run**.

Figure 218 Running an Azure function manually

```
2018-10-08T19:09:45 Welcome, you are now connected to log-streaming service.
2018-10-08T19:10:00.005 [Info] Function started (Id=b2650ab8-9fb7-4c4b-ac11-b93fcb20701f)
2018-10-08T19:10:00.005 [Info] The Total Count of Customer register as of 10/8/2018 7:10:00 PM is 3
2018-10-08T19:10:00.005 [Info] C# Timer trigger function executed at: 10/8/2018 7:10:00 PM
2018-10-08T19:10:00.005 [Info] Function completed (Success, Id=b2650ab8-9fb7-4c4b-ac11-b93fcb20701f,
Duration=13ms)
2018-10-08T19:11:45  No new trace in the past 1 min(s).
2018-10-08T19:12:45  No new trace in the past 2 min(s).
2018-10-08T19:13:45  No new trace in the past 3 min(s).
2018-10-08T19:14:45  No new trace in the past 4 min(s).
2018-10-08T19:15:00.012 [Info] Function started (Id=e30e2a5c-ff27-4855-aee0-1f50b1c32c2b)
2018-10-08T19:15:00.074 [Info] The Total Count of Customer register as of 10/8/2018 7:15:00 PM is 3
2018-10-08T19:15:00.074 [Info] C# Timer trigger function executed at: 10/8/2018 7:15:00 PM
2018-10-08T19:15:00.074 [Info] Function completed (Success, Id=e30e2a5c-ff27-4855-aee0-1f50b1c32c2b,
Duration=63ms)
2018-10-08T19:16:45  No new trace in the past 1 min(s).
2018-10-08T19:17:45  No new trace in the past 2 min(s).
2018-10-08T19:18:45  No new trace in the past 3 min(s).
2018-10-08T19:19:46  No new trace in the past 4 min(s).
2018-10-08T19:20:00.019 [Info] Function started (Id=31c5d469-f74b-4e76-844b-dc9ca0a0c34c)
2018-10-08T19:20:00.026 [Info] The Total Count of Customer register as of 10/8/2018 7:20:00 PM is 3
2018-10-08T19:20:00.026 [Info] C# Timer trigger function executed at: 10/8/2018 7:20:00 PM
2018-10-08T19:20:00.026 [Info] Function completed (Success, Id=31c5d469-f74b-4e76-844b-dc9ca0a0c34c,
Duration=7ms)
2018-10-08T19:21:46  No new trace in the past 1 min(s).
2018-10-08T19:22:46  No new trace in the past 2 min(s).
```

Figure 219 Azure function live streaming logs

References

Following are some excellent websites which you can use for more in-depth knowledge of Microsoft Azure:

- https://www.michaelcrump.net/azure-tips-and-tricks-complete-list/: Michael Crump Works at Microsoft on Azure, I personally always read his blog and had started from here. Lots of cool stuff.

- http://www.cloudranger.net/ : Cloud Ranger is a blog about the cloud offering from Microsoft known as *Microsoft Azure*. This blog offers tutorials about Microsoft Azure cloud platform free for personal consumption.

- https://docs.microsoft.com/en-us/azure/ : This site contains all documentation of Azure. I have personally read a lot from these docs when I started working on Microsoft Azure.

- https://medium.com/@jeffhollan: Jeff Hollan is senior PM Lead for Microsoft Azure Functions; you can find his blog on medium.

- https://azure.microsoft.com/en-in/resources/samples/?sort=0 : Sample projects on any of the services.

- https://github.com/Azure-Samples/ : Microsoft Azure code samples and examples in .NET, Java, Python, Node.js, PHP, and Ruby.

- I will recommend watching channel 9 episode on Azure Friday.

- If You like to listen to podcast I will recommend Microsoft Cloud Show by Andrew Connel and Chris Johnson, The Azure Podcast by Cake Teeter, Evan Basilik, and Russel Young & Sujit D'Mello and last not the least Azure Friday.

You can follow some people on Twitter which have exceptional knowledge on Microsoft Azure who are easily reachable and are always ready to help:

- *@gregor_suttie* => Gregor Suttie
- *@mbcrump* => Michael Crump
- *@Mike_kaufmann* => Mike Kaufmann
- *@codespaien* => Fabio Cavalcante
- *@jeffhollan* => Jeff Hollan
- *@scottjduffy* => Scott duffy

- *@TechTrainerTim* => Tim Warner

For Code References you can download the source code from the following link:

https://github.com/SailleshPawar/azureStepByStep

Made in the USA
Middletown, DE
08 September 2020